Motorcyclist's Guide to Travel

Motorcyclist's Guide to Travel

Mario Orsini

ISBN-13: 978-0692858035

ISBN-10: 0692858032

All photos are provided by the author unless otherwise noted:

Cannon, D. 59

Acknowledgements

I want to thank my parents for allowing me to get started in motorcycling at such a young age. Mom wasn't thrilled but she was supportive when Dad came home with a dust-covered Honda C70 for me to ride. It wasn't my dream bike but it had two wheels and a motor so it was good enough for me. That old bike started my adventures in motorcycling. I still have it to this day and it always brings a smile to my face when I ride it.

My girlfriend, Kristen also deserves some major kudos. There aren't many people in the world who would not only agree to but also enjoy riding on the back of a motorcycle clear across the country. It sure does make the trips much more enjoyable when she comes along.

After hearing the stories about my uncle's great motorcycle adventures and seeing all of the unbelievable photos, I knew at a very young age that I too wanted to travel on my motorcycle. I want to give a big thank you to my Uncle Brian for inspiring me to travel on a motorcycle.

Any finally, I need to give a huge thanks to my long-time friend Justin Ruble. We've been friends since we were 5 years old, college roommates and have so many crazy stories, you probably wouldn't believe half of them. I want to thank him for helping me edit this book. *Motorcyclist's Guide to Travel* would not have been possible without his contributions.

For a **FREE** training video to learn how I use Google Maps to help track my travel ideas, be sure to visit:

http://2wheeledrider.com/google

Table of Contents

Intro

Motorcycles are sold every day to people who dream about riding their new bikes all across the country. Unfortunately, many of those same bikes face a fate no motorcycle should ever face; they sit in the garage and are seldom ridden. There are many reasons owners don't ride their bikes more often ranging from imperfect weather to not enough time. Another reason many riders never take that big motorcycle trip they've always dreamed of is because they simply don't know where to begin.

I am fortunate to have an uncle with decades of motorcycle travel experience to bounce ideas and routes off of when I begin planning my larger trips. He's like a walking US travel encyclopedia. Since you can't buy my uncle from Amazon, I thought I would do the next best thing and write this book instead.

What you'll get from the book

This book will provide you with the information you'll need to not only plan but also execute a fun and successful motorcycle trip. I'm sharing with you the exact same methods and processes I use when I plan my own trips. Don't worry if you don't yet own a motorcycle; I'm going to cover the different types of bikes and what to look for when purchasing new or used. For those of you who already have motorcycles, you'll find plenty of information about riding gear as well as upgrades and modifications you can do to your bike to make it more "touring worthy."

Many of my trips often have a "big" destination such as the Grand Canyon or Mount Rushmore. However, during the course of a trip I may spend less than 1% of my time there. In this book I will show you how to fill in the other 99% of your trip. I will share with you some ideas of places you can travel and how to come up with your own ideas as well.

Nearly half of the book covers planning and preparing for your motorcycle trip. I go into great detail about the planning process including things like where to get started, avoiding pitfalls, how to plan out routes and much more. The book will cover final preparations for your trip including information on preparing your bike, what to pack, and additional last minute items.

I don't just show you how to plan a trip and then leave you all by yourself. We cover things you need to be doing during your trip each day like pre-ride inspections, tips on how to keep your bike safe and more. You'll also find information about what to do once you return home. And finally we will cover a hodgepodge of motorcycle travel tips, tricks and hacks I've learned along the way.

What this book does NOT cover

Since I stay at hotels and motels when I travel, this book does not provide any camping information. If you want to camp on your trip, I think you'll still find this book very useful but may want to check additional resources to gain more information on camping.

To date, all of my motorcycle travel has been in the U.S. so this book does not cover any information about riding in other countries. Also since it's specific to the U.S., please note I use miles instead of kilometers when referring to speed or distance. Even if you're located overseas I believe almost all of the information in this book will still be relevant.

Finally, as my motorcycle touring experience is limited to riding on the pavement, this book does not cover any off road-specific riding information. You should still find plenty of value in the book even if you plan to ride on unpaved roads.

Why I wrote this book

I really wrote this book for all the people who have the dream of riding their motorcycle on an amazing trip but need some more encouragement and/or a good place to start planning. When I began posting my motorcycle travel videos and pictures on YouTube and Facebook I started receiving emails on a weekly basis from folks that were interested in motorcycle touring but didn't know where to start. Some had motorcycles while others were just fascinated to know how someone could ride a bike so far. I still get questions from people through email, Facebook, YouTube and other social media platforms. I take the time to respond to each of them individually and still plan to continue to help in any way I can. My goal with writing this book is to reach a much larger audience than I am able to do answering individual questions. That said, if you have a question my contact information will be at the end of this intro so please don't hesitate to ask.

Warning

The entire book is based on my own personal experiences while motorcycle touring. I've provided you with the same methods, techniques and tips I use to plan and take a motorcycle trip. You may not agree with everything I've written and that's ok. I don't want anyone to think I think what I've written in this book is the gospel. Instead I look at this book as a set of guidelines. Use what you think is going to work best for you and throw out the rest. If I can get you to take a motorcycle trip and have a blast doing it, then I'll feel like I've done my job.

One last word of warning: MOTORCYCLE TOURING IS ADDICTIVE. I find that when I'm not currently on a trip, I spend most of my time thinking about or planning the next one. There are many great places to see and no better way to get there than by traveling on a motorcycle. Now, let's get to planning your motorcycle tour!

Contact Me

Have a question or comment? Please don't hesitate to contact me. I'd love to hear from you!

Mario Orsini
PO Box 64
Bunker Hill, WV 25413

2wheeledriderdotcom@gmail.com

http://www.2wheeledrider.com

Also, be sure to check out my YouTube channel http://youtube.com/c/2wheeledriderchannel for lots of great travel, how-to and other motorcycle-related videos.

Chapter 1
Why?

"Why would you want to ride your motorcycle that far?" is a question (or variation of a question) I often get asked when people find out the long trips I've taken on two wheels. "For those who understand, no explanation is needed. For those who do not understand, no explanation is possible." may be the perfect answer to that question. If you're reading this book, I assume you are a rider or at least want to be one, so most likely no explanation is needed for you. However, I would still like to attempt to answer the question.

For me, freedom is the biggest reason of all to travel via motorcycle. When traveling by car, you are confined to a space. When traveling by bus, train or plane you're confined to a space and on someone else's schedule. When you're traveling on a motorcycle, you have none of those constraints. You have the freedom to go wherever you want and be on your own schedule or no schedule at all. Riding along and see a great photo opportunity? Pull over to the side of the road and snap your picture. It's difficult to do that on a bus, train or plane, and many times it's even difficult to do that in a car.

Speaking of pulling over to the side of the road, you'll find that riding a motorcycle is going to provide you with many more opportunities to stop and see things than most other forms of transportation. Due to the relatively small size of a motorcycle it's very easy to pull it in front of a state line marker, national park sign or just about anything else you may find on your travels. Heck, I've even pulled mine over to get a picture with some wild buffaloes!

On a motorcycle you're going to see some amazing sights. During your entire ride you'll have a 180° unobstructed view. You can enjoy the beautiful scenery all day. It's the type of view that you just can't get on a bus or train and it's even hard to get close with a car.

You can get off the busy highway, have fun, see more and still cover plenty of miles. The highway has its purpose, but I'd much rather ride on a nice winding road. Coming upon a tractor or slow-moving vehicle on a two lane road while riding your motorcycle typically won't cause the same type of delay you'd possibly face as if you were driving a car or on a bus. State and secondary routes will have you passing by many interesting things that popular websites or guidebooks used for research may have missed. You'll find better places to eat, as many of restaurants listed on the highway exit signs are chain restaurants.

Another thing that'll be easier to do while not traveling the highway is meeting the locals. You'll be surprised how many people will strike up a conversation with you just because you're on a motorcycle. Some people you'll talk with will be riders and others will just be curious. They get especially curious when they see an out-of-state tag on the back and realize you're over 1,000 miles from home. I've had many great conversations with complete strangers while traveling on my motorcycle. Locals are also a great source of information and may point you toward a great restaurant or watering hole.

One of the least important reasons to travel by motorcycle is because it costs less. It's not a great surprise that motorcycles use less fuel than your average car. You can also pick up used motorcycles on the cheap. I've bought two reliable, street-legal motorcycles for under $1,000 each. You'd be hard pressed to buy a reliable car for under $1,000. In addition to the fuel savings and low cost of entry, you can strap some camping gear on your bike and save tons of money on lodging as well. I prefer hotels but there is something about the idea of camping that I find exciting.

Aside from the freedom, I like being a part of the elements. In a car, bus or train you don't have to deal with the wind. If it rains, you simply turn on your windshield wipers. If it gets hot, you turn on the A/C. Cold? Turn up the heat. If you see a wild bear next to the road, just roll up your window. On the bike, however, it's a totally different story. There are times the wind will beat the crap out of you! If it rains, you get wet (or put on your rain suit). If it's get hot, you sweat and if it gets cold so do you (though I have some tips on how to deal with this later in the book). And finally, if you see a wild bear next to the road, you may need a change of underwear.

When the weather is beautiful, being a part of the elements can turn a good ride into a great ride. When the weather is less than ideal or downright horrible, you may not enjoy the ride quite as much in the moment. But, you will still end up with a great story. If your idea of a great time is flying first class to a tropical island, spending your day on white sandy beaches drinking daiquiris, swimming with the dolphins, and concluding your day by having dinner cooked by a celebrity chef before retiring to your suite at a 5-star resort, then traveling on a motorcycle may not be for you. If however the idea of riding your motorcycle for hundreds of miles through 20-50° fluctuations in temperature in all types of weather, seeing some beautiful places, meeting interesting people, trying out the local hole-in-the-wall restaurant before retiring to your "clean and comfortable" room for the night to clean all the bugs and dirt off of your riding gear then taking a shower to wash the exhaust smell off of yourself before doing it all again tomorrow, then I think you're going to enjoy traveling on your motorcycle and I hope you enjoy the rest of the book.

Don't go on a vacation; go on an adventure. – Mario Orsini

Chapter 2
Travel Ideas and How to Track Them

There's a lot to do before taking off on your first motorcycle trip. While I'm sure you may already have some great ideas of where you'd like to ride your motorcycle, I'm also certain you may need a little help if you are a motorcycle adventure virgin. For those that already have some ideas or a destination in mind, I think you'll still find this chapter very informative.

You've heard the old adage, "it's not the destination, it's the journey" and that's certainly true when traveling on a motorcycle. On most of my trips, I have multiple points of interest I want to see before I get to my destination. In many cases my destination is just the nearest town with lodging to the final point of interest for the day or on a trip lasting more than 2 days, it may just be another stop along the way which will allow me to get to another point of interest the next day. The point I'm trying to make is sometimes the destination isn't very important.

In this chapter, I'm going to discuss some different types of places or things you can check out on your rides. I'm going to give you some sources to help you come up with ideas. I'm also going to give you some tips on how to store these ideas so you don't forget about them. Later in the book, I'll show you how to take all these great ideas you've come up with and turn them into a great ride.

Types

There are probably hundreds of different types of things to see on your trips so don't think the following list is exhaustive. I just want to give you a good baseline to get started.

Roads

Roads? Yes, specific roads for many riders can be the highlight of the trip. Some of them you've most certainly heard of such as U.S. 1 to the Florida Keys. While it may not be the typical motorcycle road with a bunch of curves (in fact it's pretty much just straight), you'll see some of the prettiest water in the world and get to pass over the 7 Mile Bridge. The Blue Ridge Parkway stretching from Virginia down to the Carolinas is another great road with lots of great scenery and fortunately quite a few curves. While perhaps not as popular or well known to the general public, mention *The Dragon* or *Tail of the Dragon* to most any motorcyclist and their eyes will light up. The *Tail of the Dragon* is a mountain pass between North Carolina and Tennessee that boasts 318 curves in 11 miles. While officially named U.S. 129, it's become internationally famous to sports car enthusiasts and motorcycle riders alike. There are many other great roads throughout the U.S. as well. A great road could be your destination or just a point of interest along the way.

Marker sign at Deals Gap, Home of the Dragon

Riding the Blue Ridge Parkway with family in 2004

National Parks

We are fortunate in the U.S. to have many great national parks. As of 2016, we have 59 national parks operated by the National Park Service. As of the date of publication, I've only been to 7 of them, including the South Dakota Badlands, the Grand Canyon, Grand Teton, Great Smoky Mountains, Shenandoah, Theodore Roosevelt and Yellowstone. California has the most at nine, followed by Alaska (eight), Utah (five) and Colorado (four).

Yellowstone National Park East Entrance Sign

National Monuments

In 1906, President Theodore Roosevelt established Devils Tower as the first national monument. As of 2016, there are 123 U.S. national monuments. National Monuments are located in 31 states as well as in the District of Columbia. Arizona has the greatest number with 18, followed by California with 15 and New Mexico with 14.

Devils Tower

National Forests

The U.S. has 154 National Forests covering more than 188 million acres. Alaska has the most national forest land with nearly 22 million acres, followed by California with almost 21 million acres and Idaho not far behind. In fact, Idaho has the greatest percentage of national forest land with 38.2%. Chances are you have a national forest in your state or the state next to you, as only 10 states are without a national forest.

State Parks

As of 2016, there were 6,624 state parks in the U.S. California tops the list with 278. Niagara Falls State Park is generally regarded as the oldest park in the U.S., though other states may argue. I've been to and through too many state parks to count. My home state of West Virginia has 36 state parks covering more than 75,000 acres.

Custer State Park in South Dakota (yes, those are buffaloes)

Specific States

Many motorcyclists have the goal to ride in the continental 48 states or ride to all 49 states (that you can ride to). Some want to ride in all 50 states, though you're going to have to take a ship or plane to Hawaii.

Historical Sites/Towns

Historical sites make for some great rides. Maybe you want to see the famous OK Corral where the Earp Brothers and Doc Holliday took on the infamous Cowboys, or perhaps you're a civil war buff who's always wanted to see the Gettysburg National Military Park. When it comes to historical sites, the U.S. has a lot to offer. In some instances, the entire town is historic such as the town of Williamsburg, VA. If you're into a specific time period in history, a historical destination could make for a fun motorcycle trip.

Restaurants

Make no mistake, Anthony Bourdain's former show, *No Reservations,* was a travel show first and a food show second. If you're a fan of Bourdain, Adam Richman, Guy Fieri or any other food personality, then perhaps a ride revolving around *Diners, Drive-In's and Dives* would make for a great trip. Even if you're not going to revolve your whole trip around a certain restaurant, I would still recommend researching some restaurants in the areas you'll be passing through and staying during your trip. I have nothing against chain restaurants, but I can eat at those any day of the week. When I'm in an area I've never been, I like to check out the local offerings.

Breweries

If you like beer (and I don't know many people who don't), then a trip to a brewery can be a really fun time. According to craftbeer.com, the average American lives within 10 miles of a brewery. Many breweries offer a tour in which they show you how their beer is made. Some tours are free while others may have a small fee involved. But, on almost all tours, you'll get to sample the product at the end. Another great thing about most craft breweries is they aren't located in metropolitan areas. Most are located in more rural areas which translate to a better riding experience.

Thad and I visiting Yuengling Brewery in Pottsville, PA

Distilleries

If you're a fan of distilled spirits, I'd suggest you put the Kentucky Bourbon Trail on your list of places to ride. It'll take you a few days to complete the entire trail, but you'll get to see the distilleries of Jim Beam, Maker's Mark, Woodford Reserve and many more. Again, most of these places are in rural areas that make for great scenery and a fun ride. Along the tours of the distilleries you'll get to see the bourbon (or whatever type of spirit they distill) throughout the entire process. Some will even let you bottle some yourself. Kentucky isn't the only place to find distilleries, as there are quite a few micro distilleries throughout the U.S. plus a pretty big distillery in Lynchburg, TN you may have heard of as well.

Jim Beam Distillery

Factory Tours

I've been on a few factory tours. Some are fascinating while others are duds. One of the most disappointing tours I've taken was the Ben & Jerry's Factory Tour. The only redeeming part was you got to eat ice cream at the end. There are many great factory tours available in the U.S. including the Ford Rouge Factory Tour in Dearborn, MI or the Harley Davidson factory in York, PA. Factory Tours are just another possible point of interest for your next ride. Factorytoursusa.com is a great resource for finding and researching factory tours.

TV/Movie Sites or Filming Locations

Ever wonder what happened to the baseball players in *Field of Dreams* when they walk into the corn? You can ride to Dyersville, IA to found out for yourself since the field is real. Visiting a TV or movie filming location can be a lot of fun. I've been to the *Field of Dreams* baseball field, Gold & Silver Pawn from *Pawn Stars*, and the Ohio State Reformatory, better known as Shawshank Prison. If you're a big fan of a particular TV show or movie, traveling to some of the filming locations can be a lot of fun and give you greater context the next time you watch it.

Kristen in Iowa at Field of Dreams

Museums

If you have an interest in something, then chances are a museum about that topic exists. While most have heard of the Smithsonian or the American Museum of Natural History, there are a lot of obscure museums for which you may not be familiar. Los Angeles has the Museum of Death while Gatlinburg, TN possesses the Salt & Pepper Shaker Museum. And yes, in Felton, CA, you'll find the Bigfoot Discovery Museum. For motorcycle

fans, the Barber Motorsports Museum in Birmingham, AL is
unrivaled.

Motorcycle Rallies

   While it's not my thing, motorcycle rallies are certainly very
popular. Daytona Bike Week and Sturgis are the two largest.
The Wing Ding and Myrtle Beach Bike Week are also well
attended.

Random Stuff

   While I'm not going to hop on my bike and ride 300 miles just
to see a Giant Coffee Pot, I will stop by it on my way to
somewhere else. I love stopping by to see crazy-looking oddities
along the road. Cadillac Ranch is literally just some old Cadillacs
buried hood first in the ground. So, why stop? Simple. It makes
for a great picture. Having a bunch of fun pictures of either you
or your bike standing next to some crazy landmark is a great
conversation starter and fun to share with your friends, family
and other riders.

Cadillac Ranch in Amarillo, Texas

Ideas

Ideas can come from just about anywhere. The following are a few mediums you may utilize to help you mine a few travel ideas.

Television

Channels such as the Travel Channel and History Channel are going to provide you with many different ideas and areas to travel. Be sure to pay close attention to any restaurants, bars, hotels or other points of interest that may be mentioned during the broadcast, as having this information will become valuable when it comes to planning your trip.

Magazines

Do you fly often? If so, take the time to flip through those magazines in the back of the seat in front of you. They always have great write-ups of different cities or destinations throughout the country. I've found them to be a valuable source of travel ideas. In addition to those magazines, travel magazines, motorcycle magazines, motorcycle travel magazines and even magazines on any subject you may enjoy are also valuable. A couple of my favorite magazines are *Rider* and *RoadRunner*. Both are motorcycle travel magazines that include all sorts of fun rides and destinations, many of which are provided by the readers who write guest columns. Sometimes you'll also find some freebie magazines that are mostly glorified advertising in some areas. They too can give you some great ideas.

Rest Stop Brochures

While you can also find them in some restaurants and most hotels, you will always find travel or destination brochures at rest stops. I recommend taking a couple of minutes to take a quick look and grab a couple of them that pique your interest. Once you get home, you can perform a little more research and decide if it's a place you'd like to visit. One of the best things about these brochures is they're FREE!

Books

There are thousands of books written on travel. Some are very broad but most are very specific. I've read some motorcycle-specific travel books that I've found to be both helpful and fun to read. While we're currently just talking about getting ideas on where to travel, books can also be very helpful once you've narrowed down your choices, and they can provide a lot of specific information on an area.

News Articles

Sometimes while getting the morning news on the internet, I'll come across an article such as "The Coolest Place to Visit in Each State" or something of that nature. I enjoy reading or clicking through these articles to find fun places to travel.

Travel Bloggers and Travel Vloggers

Before I explain this one, let me share that a Blogger is someone who writes stories or articles while a Vlogger is someone who tells stories through video. Travel bloggers and vloggers are people who share stories of their travel. I'm not going to name any specific ones, but seek out people online that are doing what you'd like to do and check out their blog posts or videos. I believe you'll find content that's both informative and fun.

Travel Websites

There are thousands of travel websites providing you all sorts of information and ideas. One of the questions I often get is, "how do you find these crazy things on your trips?" I love to find random oddities on my trips. I mainly do this for two purposes: 1) they make for great pictures and 2) they break up the ride a bit. My favorite website to find random oddities and roadside attractions is roadsideamerica.com. It's an amazing site that's fairly easy to navigate and constantly updated by readers. Roadtrippers.com and Atlasobscura.com are also good resources to find random oddities.

Word of Mouth

Do you know someone who already does what you want to do? Talk to them. They've "been there and done that" and will have a lot of information to share with you based on their own first-hand experiences. I'm fortunate to have an uncle that's ridden motorcycles hundreds of thousands of miles throughout the U.S. He's like a walking encyclopedia and the perfect source for me to consult with when I start planning my trips. With that said, they don't always have to be experienced motorcycle travelers, they could just be experienced travelers. It's always good to consult with someone you know who's been to an area.

Past Trips

If you're reading this book, you may not have taken any sort of trip yet but I still feel this needs to be mentioned. Once you start traveling on your bike, you're going to see things along the way that you'd really like to check out but you just don't have the time because you have already planned to see other things. Don't let this discourage you. You can always come back. I've traveled to many places only to find out about something I didn't know existed. I try to make it a point to come back to that place when I have the opportunity.

Keeping Track of your Ideas

There are many ways to track your travel ideas and research. The following are some the methods I have found most useful.

Capture the Idea (any way you can)

You never know when a great idea is going to come along so be ready to capture it; otherwise, you'll surely forget it. Post-it notes, cocktail napkins, receipts or any other piece of paper is fine for writing down an idea. Stick it in your wallet and then add it to your notebook (which I'll touch on next) or whatever tracking method you're using. Your cell phone is another great way to capture information. You can do it by snapping a picture or by using a notes app.

Notebook

Get yourself a cheap notebook and write your ideas down. I have a few notepads and notebooks with all sorts of ideas written in them. I usually write down the name of the place and any information I have about it. Sometimes it's just a name or a website with a note to research it more later. I'm sure there are better ways to organize things, but I just write an idea down when I'm thinking of it so I don't forget it. I love going back through my notebooks when it comes time to plan a trip.

Mobile Device

While the notebook is still my favorite way to keep track of my ideas, a mobile device or devices will also work. You can use a word processor app or a spreadsheet to keep track of your ideas. The nice thing about using a mobile device is you can also put in clickable links to quickly access websites. I would recommend using a cloud-based service like Google Drive so you can access your information from any mobile device or computer. It also makes it very easy to share with friends and family that may be joining you.

Computer

You can create a desktop folder to hold all of your information and documentation you've collected on your travel ideas. Like with mobile devices, you can also have clickable links in your documents so you can quickly access different websites. You may also want to create a bookmark folder in your favorite web browser for quick access to your favorite websites as well.

Google Maps

Aside from my notebook, Google Maps is my favorite tool for keeping track of my travel destinations. With Google Maps you can create your own custom maps with your specific points of interest pinned on them. I've created a handful of motorcycle maps. Because they're on Google, you can log into any mobile device or computer to access your Maps. I like to create different maps. I also have one called "Motorcycle Day Trips" which includes places that are within a day's ride. Once I've visited the place, I take it off the map. My *day trips* map is constantly being updated throughout the year.

Compile Your Ideas

I want to end this chapter by stressing the importance of tracking your ideas. As I've discussed I have multiple ways I track my trip ideas. You can use all, some or none of my ideas as long as you don't rely on the "I'll store it in my head" strategy. Your ideas and preliminary research need to be written down and tracked either in hardcopy or soft copy form. The more ideas, information and research you gather the easier and quicker it'll be to plan your trip.

Compiling your ideas isn't something you really need to spend much time doing. In most cases, I jot down a quick note in my notebook or on a slip of paper. When I have some spare time or feel inclined to research the point of interest a little more, I may spend a few minutes researching it on my phone or computer again taking a few notes or maybe just screenshotting a website or address. When it comes time to plan my trip, I gather up my notes and have a great starting point to begin planning.

Chapter 3
The Bike

Spoiler alert: I'm not going to tell you what type of bike to buy. Buying a motorcycle is a very personal choice and in most cases a pretty big financial commitment. However, I'm going to do the best I can to assist you in finding the right type of bike for you.

What Type of Riding

What type of riding you want to do is a question only you can answer. It's also a question in which you need to be totally honest with yourself. You don't want to end up with the wrong bike. Are you planning to do a lot of commuting on the bike? Do you want to take a really big trip or maybe just some overnighters? Will you be doing all your miles on pavement or will you venture off road as well? Are you going to be riding solo or two-up? These are just a few examples of questions you need to ask yourself when trying to decide what type of riding you will be doing.

Budget

As with most things, you can spend a small amount of money on a motorcycle or as much as you want or can. It's possible to pick up a great used bike for a few thousand dollars or you can spend tens of thousands on an exotic or custom motorcycle. The choice is yours.

In addition to the upfront cost of the bike, there are many other things to consider when it comes to your budget.

Insurance

There are too many variables to list when it comes to insurance prices, but you'd be well-advised to get a few quotes before making a purchase. Generally speaking, sportbikes cost more to insure than any other type of motorcycle; and sorry young rider, you're going to be paying more than those your senior. I bought a new 2003 Honda CBR600 F4i for around $7,300 when I was 21 years old. The best price I could get on full coverage insurance was $3,400 a year! Fortunately I paid cash, so I could just put liability on it which was about $30 a month. At the time of this book's publication, I'm 35 years old and most bikes cost me $30 or less a month for a full coverage policy. As you can see, there's a big difference between paying $300 a month versus $30 a month. It's best to check *before* making a purchase.

Maintenance

Are you a take-it-to-the-dealer person or a do-it-yourselfer? If you can do most of the maintenance work yourself, it's going to save you a TON of money. I'm not going to get on my soapbox about how you should work on your bike, but I will say none of my bikes have ever been to a dealer or a mechanic. I have nothing against mechanics or dealers; I just prefer to work on my own equipment.

One of the biggest recurring costs on a motorcycle is tires. Motorcycle tires normally last anywhere from 3,000 miles to over 20,000 miles. Though tire prices vary greatly, you can generally expect to pay around $200 retail for a name-brand street front tire and $250-300 for a rear. To get the tires mounted and balanced, you can expect to pay anywhere from $50 to more than $100 a tire. Some shops will cut you a break and charge about half of the normal mount and balance fee if you bring your wheels in already off the bike (yet another reason to learn to work on your own bike). If you know how (and have the tools) to mount and balance your own tires, you could order them from a discount retailer which will save you anywhere from 20-40% and save the service costs. Instead of paying around $700 at a shop, you could do it yourself and keep an extra $400 in your pocket.

Oil changes are a relatively easy thing to do that require a minimal number of tools and can also save you a lot of money if you do it yourself. On most bikes, it takes me less time to get out my tools, change the oil and filter, and put everything away than it does to ride to the dealer and back.

The other big cost when it comes to maintaining your motorcycle will be the service intervals. While it varies for every bike, at some point a valve clearance check and/or adjustment is going to be necessary. If popping the valve cover off of your engine scares you, then it's best to take it back to the dealer or to a motorcycle mechanic to have them perform the service for you. Service intervals like these will generally run a few hundred dollars because there are quite a few labor hours involved. When researching bikes, be sure to find out what the service intervals are and then check around to find out what it's going to cost you to have it done.

Gear

While I will go into more detail on riding gear in a later chapter, it needs to be mentioned now as it can affect your budget when purchasing a bike. At minimum, I would budget money for a good helmet, riding gloves, and a jacket. In a perfect world, a nice pair of riding boots and some good riding pants would be nice to have as well. However, if you're tight on funds, a pair of over the ankle work boots and jeans will hold you over until you can get some better gear. How much should you spend? As much as you can reasonably afford. At absolute minimum, plan on spending about $40 for gloves, $100 for a jacket and $150 for a helmet.

New or Used

In the next two sections, I'll discuss the pros and cons of buying a new or used motorcycle. Some riders will only buy new for "peace of mind," while others prefer to buy used to save some money. I've bought both new and used motorcycles, so I want to share with you my thoughts on the topic.

Buying a Used Bike

I've purchased over a dozen motorcycles, and only 4 of them have been new. Buying a used motorcycle can save you a lot of money, but if you don't know what to look for it can also cost you a lot of money. I could probably write an entire chapter, if not entire book, on what to look for when buying a used motorcycle. But, that's not the purpose of this book, so I'm going to keep it short and instead give you some tips.

Once you've narrowed it down to the model of bike that piques your interest, start doing your research! If a bike model exists, then so do multiple forums dedicated to that specific bike. Most forums will have a 'sticky' thread at the top with frequently asked questions, or known issues on the bike. Be sure to check those out as they will provide you with a wealth of knowledge and tell you exactly what to be on the lookout for when checking out a used bike.

When you decide to go look at a bike, take a knowledgeable friend along. Even if you already know what to look for and feel 100% confident in your abilities to check out a motorcycle, I would still take a knowledgeable friend along as he/she can be invaluable. Your friend will help you keep you from making an emotional decision. He/she is not emotionally invested in the bike, so he/she will be much more objective when checking out the bike. Your friend may also see things you may miss. Even if you're knowledgeable, you may get busy talking to the current owner and miss something. It also helps to have a second brain, because you may forget to ask an important question about the bike that your friend may remember. And most importantly, if you decide to buy the bike, your friend can help you unload it when you get home!

So in conclusion, do your research, know what to look for and take a knowledgeable friend.

Buying a New Bike

Again, I could probably write an entire chapter or book on how to buy a new motorcycle. I will once again keep it brief. Much like buying a used bike, you need to do your research. Even if the bike has only been out a short while, rest assured there is already a forum that's been formed and owners discussing any shortcomings of the bike.

Keep on the lookout for any bike shows or manufacturer demos in your area. You may be able to get a test ride with little to no pressure to buy a new bike. Read everything you can on the bike and talk to other owners. You can never have too much information.

My only other quick bit of advice is to not buy a brand new model immediately after it comes out. Give it some time to make sure there are no major issues before dropping a load of money. A few years back, BMW had a major recall on their brand new R1200RT with their new Dynamic ESA suspension package. The problem was so bad they even offered to buy the bikes back at the original purchase price AND owners received $1,000 toward another BMW motorcycle. While ultimately BMW was able to remedy the problem with the suspension and this is an extreme example, I just want to illustrate that sometimes it's better to wait a little while to let others discover the problems.

Types of Bikes

There are many different types of bikes to choose from, but I'm going to narrow them down to 8 categories. While I'm sure an argument could be made for more or less categories, I believe the following 8 should suffice. I'm only including street legal motorcycles on this list.

Standard

The Standard Motorcycle is a general purpose motorcycle. Most have a fairly upright riding position with the foot pegs below the rider and the handlebars high enough and close enough so the rider isn't leaning too far forward which leads to a pretty comfortable riding position. Standard bikes are sometimes referred to as "naked bikes" because they have little to no fairings. Standard bikes are normally on the lower end of the cost spectrum. Their engines are usually a little milder than some other types of bikes, and their suspensions usually don't offer the adjustability found on sports bikes or even tourers. Almost every major manufacturer has at least one standard motorcycle in their lineup with most having many to offer. The standard motorcycle is a very flexible bike that with a little work could become a touring bike, track bike, sport bike or just about anything else you could imagine which also explains why they are some of the best-selling motorcycles in the world.

Standard motorcycle example: Ducati Monster

Cruiser

Cruisers may be what you first picture in your mind when someone says the word motorcycle. In fact, I would venture to guess most people, in the US anyway, will think of Harley-Davidson. Most motorcycles in the cruiser category have V-twin engines tuned for lots of low end torque. The riding position will have you sitting upright or even leaned back with your feet forward and your hands fairly high. Of course, there are always exceptions, but I'm speaking in general terms. Cruisers usually have lower seat heights than most other styles of bikes. They also typically have very little ground clearance which limits their cornering ability. With the addition of soft or hard bags and the addition of a windshield, cruisers can be made into suitable touring bikes.

There are a few sub-models of cruisers including choppers or bobbers, power cruisers and baggers or dressers. A chopper usually begins its life as a cruiser but is "chopped" down by removing or shortening the fenders of the bike. When it comes to choppers or bobbers, the sky's the limit when it comes to modifications. Power cruisers are cruisers with more horsepower, upgraded brakes and suspension and more ground clearance. While still not the greatest handling bikes, these motorcycles are super-quick in a straight line and still out handle their cruiser brethren. Baggers and dressers are cruisers with hard luggage attached from the factory or dealer to make them more touring friendly.

Cruiser example: Honda Valkyrie

Power cruiser example: Yamaha VMAX

Sportbike

Sportbikes are all about acceleration, braking and handling on paved surfaces. Sportbikes in many cases are road race bikes with lights and a horn. Sportbikes have high foot pegs which keep your legs closer to your body to improve ground clearance while cornering. They also have a pretty long reach to the handlebars or clip-ons that will position the rider's body over the fuel tank. Because of these ergonomics, sport bikes aren't the most comfortable to ride, especially over longer distances.

The sportbike class is dominated by inline four-cylinder engines which are high horsepower and high revving, though Ducati and Triumph like to spice things up a bit producing their bikes with twin and triple cylinder engines respectively. With very few exceptions, sport bikes are chain driven and have full fairings.

Streetfighters are a subset of the sportbike category. Streetfighters are usually based on a sportbike but have had the fairings removed, handlebars placed higher and usually the engines have been retuned for more midrange power. They are sportier than standard bikes but not as sporty as sportbikes.

Sportbike example: Honda CBR500

Dual Sport

Dual Sports are basically street legal dirt bikes. They usually have single cylinder engines ranging from 250-650cc, minimal bodywork, large front wheel, high handlebars, long, flat seats, spoked wheels, crash protection and high ground clearance. Due to their lightweight, high ground clearance, and durability dual sports are great off road. They can handle the toughest of terrain and are much less likely than other bikes to get damaged when crashed or dropped. When one is dropped, they are pretty easy to pick up since they are so light. Dual sports usually have long production runs, so finding parts is not difficult and most are very easy to work on.

The one spot where dual sports fall short is highway performance. They tend to vibrate or get "buzzy" at highway speeds due to their small single cylinder engines. Most have smaller gas tanks so you can't travel far between fuel stops not that you would want to since their flat seats are not comfortable for long runs anyway. They also have very little if any wind protection and be careful of the front fender as they can get a bit "floppy" at higher speeds. Dual sports are tough to beat on winding back roads as their high ground clearance will allow you to carry plenty of speed through the corners.

A subset of the Dual Sport is the Supermoto. The Supermoto is a Dual Sport with a stiffer suspension setup for road riding and/or racing and is usually outfitted with 17" wheels front and back wrapped with street tires.

Supermoto example: Suzuki DRZ400SM

Sport Tourer

Sport touring motorcycles are a combination of sport bikes and touring bikes. The riding position is less extreme than a sport bike but in most cases it'll still have you leaning forward a bit. Your passenger will also be much more comfortable and happy for that matter. When compared to true touring bikes, sport tourers are lighter with more powerful engines, better handling suspensions and better braking. Sport tourers make excellent "canyon carvers" and still allow you to cover long distances in comfort. Sport tourers usually come with hard saddlebags or have them available as a factory option. Top cases or trunks are sometimes available as well from either the factory or aftermarket companies. Also, many sport tourers are shaft driven keeping the maintenance to a minimum.

Sport Tourer example: Yamaha FJR1300

Tourer

While most any bike can be made into a touring bike, some are built to be tourers from the start. Touring bikes have large displacement engines, large fairings and windshields giving the rider excellent weather and wind protection and large fuel tanks to allow for long stretches between fuel stops. They are the most comfortable of all motorcycle types with plush seats and great ergonomics with a comfortable upright seating position. Your passenger will likely be very happy as well as they provide more room and more comfort for passengers than most other bikes. Tourers will almost always come with a set of hard saddlebags and in most cases a top case or trunk. Sometimes they are detachable, but some have the luggage made into the design of the bike. With large engines, large fuel tanks and large fairings, tourers are the heaviest of all motorcycle categories with most weighing around 800-900 lbs and that's before adding any gear or luggage. If your goal is to cover long distances on two wheels, it's tough to top a tourer.

Tourer example: Honda Gold Wing

Adventure Bike

If you're like me, when you hear adventure bike or adventure tourer you instantly have Ewan McGregor and Charley Boorman pop into your head. While adventure bikes have been around for over 30 years, it was these two that made them famous with *Long Way Round* and *Long Way Down*. Adventure bikes usually have 650cc or larger engines, large fuel tanks, windscreens, good ground clearance and long suspension travel, some sort of luggage system, protective guards to prevent off-road damage and a comfortable riding position. These bikes can run highway speeds all day long with some of them making more power than sport bikes. They can be quite a bit heavier off road than your typical dual sport with some weighing as much as 500 lbs or more. Some adventure bikes have complex engines and advanced electronics which can make them difficult to fix when in a remote area. They are also some of the more expensive bikes on the market.

Adventure Bike example: KTM 1290 Super Adventure

Conclusion

Armed with the information I've provided in this chapter, you should be able to start to narrow your research on the type of bike you want to purchase. Check out the forums and talk to other riders. If a motorcycle show is coming to your area, GO! You'll have the opportunity to see many bikes up close and even be able to throw a leg over them without being hassled to buy one. Some shows offer demo rides, so be sure to check ahead of time as you may be able to take some bikes out for a quick spin. If not, keep a look out for manufacturer demos coming to your area. Best of luck with your purchase.

If you already have a motorcycle, congrats! Now, flip to the next chapter. We still have a lot of work to do to prepare for your first big trip!

Chapter 4
Gear

If you've been riding motorcycles for a while then chances are that you'll already have all or at least most of the necessary gear I'm about to cover. In some states there are laws requiring some of this gear and in some it's totally optional. Please check the laws in your state.

Helmets

A good helmet is the single most important piece of riding gear every motorcyclist should have. I'm sure you're all aware that riders wearing helmets are much less likely to suffer serious head injuries when involved in an accident. However, there are a few other reasons to wear a helmet while riding.

Many states have laws requiring you to wear a helmet, so owning one (and wearing it) is a necessity if you're planning to travel throughout the U.S. While it will depend on individual insurance companies, not wearing a helmet could result in higher premiums. One advantage to wearing a helmet not many riders think about is that it makes you more visible. More visibility on a motorcycle is always a good thing. A helmet is great at protecting you from bugs and other road debris you're going to face on longer rides. I personally wear a full face helmet and sometimes have to clean the bugs off multiple times a day on longer rides. I'd much rather have to clean off my helmet than have all of those bugs hitting me in the face. And finally, a helmet can protect you from the elements. The sunshine may feel good for a while but after a few hours in the saddle sunburn and windburn can become a big problem. Also, it's not much fun getting pelted in the face or on top of your head by rain at 70 mph.

You should always try on helmets before buying one. Most motorcycle shops will have someone on hand that can help you with the proper fitment. When trying on a helmet, it should be snug around any part of your head that would be covered by a baseball cap. It shouldn't be any tighter than a beanie (knitted winter cap) would fit. It should be slightly compressed but should not be squeezing your head or painful in any way. There also shouldn't be any specific points where you feel pressure such as your forehead, back of your head or your temples. The helmet should be tightly compressed around your cheeks. While this area may be slightly uncomfortable at first, it will break in over time.

There are three main helmet safety standards. In the U.S., the helmet must be Department of Transportation (DOT) certified. DOT standards are aimed at protecting skulls from 90% of impact types and favors a more shock-absorbent helmet. The Snell Memorial Foundation is a non-profit, independent organization established in 1957 and named after William Snell, a race car driver who was killed in 1956 when his helmet failed to protect his head during an accident. The old Snell M2005 standard favored a more shock-resistant helmet but the newer M2010 standard prefers more shock-absorbent helmet like the DOT standard. The United Nations Economic Commission for Europe developed the ECE R22-05 standard which is approved for all major motorcycle racing competitions including MotoGP. It is most in common with the DOT standard and is considered the most up-to-date certification standard.

Now that we've discussed the importance of wearing a helmet, how one should fit, and the different safety ratings, let's move on to the different types of helmets available on the market.

Helmet Types

I've narrowed down the types of helmets to just three categories: full face, ¾ and ½. There are numerous subsets and variations. When it comes to full face helmets, I recommend trying on a lot of different helmets to find the type, style and size that works best for you.

Full Face

As I stated earlier, I prefer a full face helmet. There is a reason why MotoGP, Motocross and every other racer wears a full face helmet; it provides the most protection in case of accident, from road debris and from the elements. It will also muffle out more wind noise than any other type of helmet. Prices of full face helmets vary greatly and range from $40 to $800 or more. Expect to pay at least $100 for a decent quality full face helmet. Helmet prices vary due to materials used to make the helmet, weight, brand, ventilation, paint scheme and other factors. Arguably the top two brands are Arai and Shoei. I've owned both, and they both make excellent helmets.

A subset of full face helmets is the dual sport helmet. The dual sport helmet is a combination of a full face street helmet and a motocross or dirt bike helmet. It will have a flip down shield like a standard full face but also features a visor (like a dirt bike helmet), but it's made to be more aerodynamic for high speeds. Arai invented this type of helmet with their XD. Since its introduction, many manufacturers are now producing dual sport helmets.

One more type of full face helmet which has become more popular in recent years is the modular helmet. A modular or "flip up" helmet is a helmet that looks like a traditional full face helmet, but you can flip up the chin bar and face shield exposing your face similar to a ¾ helmet. Modular helmets allow long distance guys to get a drink or a quick bite to eat without having to take off their helmets. Most modular helmets also have an internal sunshield that allow you to flip a lever and provide you with instant shielding from the sun without having to carry an additional face shield.

3/4 Helmet

A 3/4 helmet covers the top and sides of your head but keeps your face exposed. 3/4 helmets can be worn with or without a face shield. Most can also be outfitted with a headset.

1/2 Helmet

A 1/2 helmet covers the top of your head and that's about it. Normally they are worn with goggles or glasses.

Jacket/Pants/Suit

A good riding jacket or suit can go a long way to support making your trip more enjoyable while keeping you comfortable and safe. A quality, proper-fitting riding jacket can help protect you from the elements, road debris and keep you better protected in the event of a crash. Riding jackets can cost as little as $100 or over $1,000. As with most things, you get what you pay for, but in most cases, you can find a quality jacket for about $200.

Types of Jackets

There are lot of things to think about when deciding on which jacket to buy. First, do NOT purchase your jacket from a department or designer clothing store. While the jacket may be labeled as a "motorcycle jacket," it's not. These are motorcycle "style" jackets that only look like motorcycle jackets but offer little or none of the protective capabilities or comfort of an actual motorcycle specific riding jacket.

A good friend of mine spent hundreds of dollars on a handful of different designer motorcycle "style" jackets only to be continually disappointed. Once up to highway speed, most of the time his jacket would blow up like a balloon because it didn't have proper ventilation. After about a year, he finally bought a proper motorcycle jacket for less than what he had spent on the other jackets that hadn't worked out. It was a good thing because shortly after purchasing the jacket he had a crash. The jacket kept him protected, and he only walked away with mild soreness. Aside from having to have a zipper replaced and a little scuffing of the leather, the jacket survived the spill as well.

No matter which type of jacket you buy, be sure it either comes with armor or has pockets for armor. Armor is like a helmet for your body. Most jackets typically have armor (or at least pockets for armor) in the shoulders, elbows (which usually covers part of the forearm) and back. The industry standard for armor is the CE standard. The CE standard for motorcycle protective gear was created by a group of industry and medical consultants in Europe. Currently, there is CE 1 rated gear which is enough to prevent broken bones in more crashes at street speeds and CE2 which will absorb 71% more energy making the armor even safer though in most cases heavier and thicker. Like motorcycle helmet safety standards, CE standards are always being updated to provide riders with the safest gear possible. I would highly recommend a jacket with CE rated armor or buying a jacket that has pockets for the armor and adding the CE rated armor of your choice.

While one could argue there are many different types of motorcycle jackets, for simplicity, I'm going to break it down into two categories: leather and textile.

Leather

When you think of a motorcycle rider or "biker," you most likely picture someone wearing a leather jacket. Leather jackets have been around a long time and continue to be the choice of jacket for many riders. Not only does leather look cool, it does a great job of keeping you protected. Leather has a very high resistance to abrasion which explains why professional motorcycle racers wear leather suits. When it gets cold outside, leather also does an excellent job of keeping you insulated from the cooler temperatures. In the event of a crash, if your leather jacket were to get damaged, in many cases it is possible to have it repaired by a leather shop, which will be a lot cheaper than having to buy a new jacket. Leather jackets can last a very long time, but they will require frequent care to keep them from drying out.

There are a few other negatives to consider about leather jackets. They cost more. A quality leather jacket will usually cost significantly more than its textile counterpart. While perforated leather jackets exist, even those will get hot in the summer time. Modern day jackets have many more vents than the jackets of yesteryear. As good as they are at keeping you warm in cooler temps, they are going to keep you even warmer when the mercury rises. Part of the reason leather jackets keep you warmer is due to their weight; they are usually heavier than textile jackets. The final knock on leather jackets is they are not waterproof. While they will likely stand up to light rain, anything more than that and you're going to have to either put on a rain suit or get wet.

Textile

Textile jackets usually have a lower cost of entry while still providing riders with lots of protection. Textile jackets are made in many different styles by almost every major manufacturer. In addition to greater affordability, textile jackets are usually lighter in weight as well. Most have lots of vents you can unzip to get the air flowing to keep you cool when the temperatures get warm. There are also mesh textile jackets, which provide tons of airflow for cooling in the summer months. Abrasion resistance comes in many different levels but most textile jackets have heavier fabric in the high impact areas (shoulders, elbows). Many of them are either treated to be waterproof or have waterproof, breathable liners so you can stay dry without the addition of a rain suit. Another great thing about textiles is they require very little care. You can wipe off the bugs and if it gets really dirty, throw it in the washer.

As with leather jackets, textile jackets have their drawbacks as well. Probably their biggest drawback is repairability. There are not many places that are going to be willing to repair your textile jacket, and matching the fabric will be nearly impossible. While it's true some manufacturers will repair them if you ship them back, in most cases it makes more financial sense to just buy a new jacket. The other big drawback of textile jackets is you're not going to look as cool wearing one of them as you would a leather jacket.

Pants

Fortunately, motorcyclists are no longer stuck wearing leather chaps over their 501s. Thanks to the many innovative motorcycle apparel companies over the last few years, we now have more choice of riding pants than ever. Many of the pants will come with a zipper on the back that will allow you to zip them onto a matching jacket and thus making it like a full riding suit. Just like the jackets, pants come in both leather and textile. Also, like the jackets, the different types of pants have the same pros and cons.

Another type of riding pants is the riding jean. Riding jeans look like regular jeans but are more abrasion resistant and cut differently. Most riding jeans are made of a heavy denim or similar material and then reinforced by Kevlar in the high impact areas. Many riding jeans also have pockets for armor in the knee area and some even in the hip area. Unlike regular jeans, riding jeans are designed to fit you best while riding the bike, so most will have stretch panels in the knees and waist to ensure maximum comfort while on the bike. If you love wearing jeans but want the protection of a riding pant, riding jeans may be for you.

Suits

If you don't want to go with a jacket and pant combo, you can choose a full riding suit. These come in leather and textile as well. While some riders will ride in full leather suits on the street, most long distance riders opt for the textile suits. Aerostich is probably the king of one-piece riding suits, but other companies make them as well. The Aerostich suit is also a favorite amongst commuters since you can wear your regular clothes underneath.

Gloves

Gloves are one of the most important things you can wear to keep you protected when riding a motorcycle. Trying to catch yourself when falling is a natural instinct. Imagine trying to catch yourself while falling off your bike on asphalt; it's not a pretty picture. In addition to protection in case of a crash or fall, gloves can also protect you from road debris. My uncle seldom wore riding gloves until a piece of debris flew off of a truck in front of him, striking his finger and cutting through the tendons. Now, he never rides without gloves. While I've never experienced anything quite that severe myself, I have had rocks, bugs and other small items hit my hands. My gloves have always done an adequate job of keeping my hands protected. Besides keeping your hands protected, gloves can also make for a more comfortable ride. A good pair of riding gloves can take some of the vibration out of your handlebars. Obviously in colder temps, a paired of lined gloves can keep your hands nice and warm.

Almost all riding gloves are made, at least in some part, of leather. Most manufacturers make riding gloves for different types of riding and different seasons or climates. It's tough to find a glove that is perfect for all types of riding and weather situations, so I have a cabinet full of different gloves. Most of them are a few years old, because they don't get worn often. I always have a favorite pair that get worn most and therefore wear out quicker than the others. I own a pair of summer riding gloves, winter riding gloves, waterproof gloves, standard gloves, and off road gloves. If you're just starting out. I would recommend deciding on what type of riding you'll be doing most and buy the glove that will best fit those circumstances. You'll have plenty of time to upgrade your riding gear later.

Boots

When it comes to riding boots, there are many different types for many different types of riding. When it comes to touring riding, I prefer a "touring" boot that is waterproof. A touring boot is a riding boot made to keep you protected in case of a crash but also provide a decent amount of comfort for walking around after dismount. The reason I prefer a waterproof boot is because riding with wet socks is absolutely no fun. My boots are Gore-Tex, but many manufacturers also offer their own waterproof, breathable version that is similar to Gore-Tex. Even though I love waterproof boots, they aren't nearly as breathable nor do they keep your feet as cool in warmer temperatures as boots with built in mesh or summer-specific boots that are made to keep you cooler.

Boots are a personal choice, and I would recommend trying them on, walking around in them and even sitting on your bike with them on before spending your hard-earned cash. As with any other type of shoe, the sizes are a good guideline but sizing varies by brand. A good boot will last you a long time, so spending the money up front is worth it.

Rain Suit

If you have purchased a waterproof jacket, pants, gloves and boots, you may not need a rain suit. However, if you have not, a rain suit can be a great investment. Like all the other gear examined, rain suits come in all sorts of price ranges. You should expect to spend in the range of $50 to a few hundred dollars. Rain suits are made to be worn over your existing riding gear. They won't provide you much protection in a crash, but they will keep you dry in the rain. If you're going to be traveling any significant distance on a motorcycle, rain gear is a must.

Final Thoughts on Riding Gear

In the past, I've always worn a full-face helmet, textile riding jacket, jeans, riding gloves, and waterproof riding boots. I have owned over-pants (riding pants to be worn over regular pants), but I only wore those when it got cold. A couple of riding seasons ago, I switched from regular jeans to riding jeans. The riding jeans were much more comfortable while riding and provided much better protection (though fortunately, I haven't had to really test them). More recently I started riding in actual (textile) riding pants. The textile riding pants are by far the most comfortable pants I've ever worn while riding and provide even more protection than regular jeans and riding jeans. I usually carry rain pants on longer trips since most of my jackets either have some sort of waterproof coating or a waterproof liner. I usually keep my waterproof gloves handy as well.

There is no perfect riding gear that's going to suit every rider. It's going to take a bit of experimentation and trial and error to find out what will work best for you. Once you find the riding gear that best suits your riding type and style, I can promise you it will make for a much more comfortable and safer riding experience.

Chapter 5
Planning

It's Time to Get Serious

Chapter 5 is probably the reason you bought this book. If you knew how to plan and complete a long distance motorcycle trip, you would have done it already. In this chapter I will share the methods I use when planning my motorcycle trips. I wish I could give you a step-by-step guide to follow, but planning a motorcycle trip is not a linear process. It's also not an easy process, but it is something I have fun doing. Let's get to planning!

Things You Will Need

You're going to need a few things to get started:

- Your list of possible travel destinations/points of interest
- Pad of paper
- Pencil (with an eraser)
- Computer or mobile device
- Atlas (Yes, an old-school atlas)

How to Begin Planning

The reason I suggest a pencil (over a pen) is because the first draft of your trip is going to be significantly different than your final draft. You are going to make a lot of changes along the way as you uncover pitfalls or discover other interesting things you want to do along the way.

Destination or Time Frame?

The planning of my motorcycle trips usually begins with one of two things: a destination or a time frame. It doesn't matter which one you start with because once you have one, the other soon follows. In some cases I may only have 3 days to ride over a long weekend, so I will begin with the time frame and figure out destinations or points of interest I can get to in the amount of time. Other times, I have a destination in mind and then figure out how long it will take me to get there and back. There are a lot of things to factor in when estimating how long it will take you to get to a certain destination, but I'm going to provide you with some tools to make it easier. Also, the more you travel on your bike, the easier it gets to get an accurate estimate.

Mileage

Before we can get to any real planning, we need to figure out how many miles you can comfortably ride your motorcycle in a given day. The easiest place to start is to figure out the longest you've ever ridden your current motorcycle in a day. Notice, I said your *current* motorcycle. It doesn't matter if you once rode your old Honda Goldwing 300 miles in a day if you now ride a Harley Sportster. If you've never ridden more than 200 miles in a day, I would suggest doing a 250-350 mile day trip before attempting any sort of overnight trip on your motorcycle. Take your highest mileage total from one day and add 10% for a good starting point for your daily mileage maximum. For example, if your highest mileage day was 250 miles, adding 10% would give you 275 miles. Use 275 miles as your maximum daily mileage gauge for planning your first trip.

Armed with the number above, you should now have a good idea of how far you can ride your motorcycle in a day. Now, we need to figure out how long it will take you to cover that distance. There are 2 main methods I use when trying to calculate how long I'll spend in the saddle each day. The first method may seem overly simplified, but it works.

All you have to do to figure out the time on your bike is assume you're going to average 50 miles per hour. Take the total mileage you want to cover and divide by 50. The number you get is the number of hours you'll be on the bike. For instance, if you're planning to ride 300 miles, you can reasonably assume it's going to take you about 6 hours. I use the rule of 50 when I'm traveling multiple types of roads such as a mixture of state routes, back roads, highways and interstates. If you're traveling almost all interstate, you can use the same calculation method but replacing the 50 with 60. I know you may be skeptical, because you know you ride faster than 50 or 60 miles per hour. But keep in mind that this estimate is taking into account barriers to speed such as stop lights, fuel stops, bathroom breaks and other hold ups along the way.

You can get an accurate estimate of how long you'll be on the bike by using Google Maps or a similar app. You can type in your destination and starting point and it will advise you exactly how long it will take to get there. Please keep in mind though, these apps don't take into account stops along the way. If you're mapping out a long route, remember most motorcycles have a shorter travel distance between fill ups than most cars.

Neither of these methods takes into account longer stops. If you're planning to go somewhere other than a food fast joint or gas station for lunch, you'll need to take that into account when planning your riding day. Also, any point of interest or other attraction you're planning to spend time at will need to be taken into account.

Time Zones

When traveling north or south, time zones will rarely be a factor. But when you're traveling east or west, times zones need to be taken into account. Time zones are important to remember for two reasons.

You need to remember to factor in time zones when it comes to operating hours of a place you may be planning to visit. You don't want to arrive an hour before the place opens because you forgot it was in another time zone. You also don't want to arrive too late and not be able to gain access.

The second reason to take time zones into account is during the initial planning of your trip. On days I'm traveling west and gaining an hour of time, I add additional mileage to the day. I truly look at it as an extra hour of time I can ride and take full advantage of it. On the flip side, when I'm traveling east and losing an hour, I plan to ride one less hour or about 50-60 less miles than on a typical day.

When you're mapping out your trip, just be cognizant of the time zones and don't forget to factor their impact.

Destination

Let's presume you're going to start out with a destination to begin planning your trip. The first thing you're going to have to do is figure out how long it's going to take you to get there. Usually, the first thing I do to get a ballpark idea is type in my home address and the destination address into Google Maps and see what figure it spits back at me. Google Maps will show you both the mileage and the estimated time. Take note that the estimated time includes current traffic time in most cases. A major metropolitan area during rush hour will factor in more traffic and a longer estimated time than it would during a weekend or off peak.

Armed with the mileage and a time estimate, you should now have a decent idea of how many hours or perhaps days it will take you to arrive at your destination. Please keep in mind, this is just a start. We'll fine tune the ride later on to make sure it includes some fun roads or other things you may want to check out along the way. It's your trip, so you can take it any way you like. This book is to give you ideas so you can use them to make the best trip for you.

Time

Another way to start planning a trip is to start with the amount of days you have to travel. Most people (unless retired or independently wealthy) are going to have some sort of restrictions on the amount of time they can take off work to take or motorcycle trip or any sort of vacation for that matter. I will sometimes look forward to holiday weekends and use them as a starting point for planning a trip. You can cover a surprising amount of miles on a three-day weekend. Sometimes I'll take the Friday off as well and turn it into a four-day trip.

When you start with a time frame, figure out how many miles you can cover in a day. Once you have a rough mileage estimate, you can use it as a radius from your home. Pull out your notes on places you'd like to visit and figure out which ones are within the mileage radius of your time frame. The ones on the outer edge will mean less stops along the way while the ones well within the radius will allow for a more leisurely ride.

Additional Considerations

Before we get into the gritty details of planning your motorcycle trip, we need to cover a few additional things you may need to consider.

Solo, Two-up, Group

Riding solo, two-up or with a group of other riders will all pose some different scenarios when it comes to planning for your trip. All three ways of travel can be enjoyable. The following are some items you should take into consideration when planning your trip.

Solo

If you're planning to do a trip by yourself, you can plan it all by yourself as well. You don't have to listen to anyone else's suggestions or ideas. That doesn't mean you can't ask a friend for suggestions or ideas, it just means you don't have to take them into consideration. On a solo trip, you can plan everything you want to do and that interests you. You also have the option to ride as many miles as you want, or can handle, each day of the trip.

Another positive about riding solo is that you don't have to share any luggage space. When I take solo trips, I use one saddlebag (though I fill both halfway for weight distribution purposes) so I have plenty of room for souvenirs or I can lock my helmet in one of the bags when I'm off the bike. The big negative to riding solo is you have to pay for the entire trip. With a passenger or in a group ride, you may be able to split up the hotel room costs.

I do have a key tip if you're planning to travel solo. When you go out to dinner, sit at the bar. Even if you don't drink alcohol, I still recommend sitting at the bar. For one thing, if the place is on a wait, you can normally find a seat at the bar and most bar seats are open seating. You'll also find other people that are traveling, usually for work, having dinner at the bar. Most are friendly, and you never know who you'll end up meeting. I've had many interesting conversations with complete strangers. If it's not crowded, most bartenders are pretty good conversationalists if you are worried about eating in complete silence. If you're not a "people person," you may still enjoy the bar more than a booth or table by yourself. Most bar seating will have a television or two to watch a game or catch up on the news or weather.

Two-Up

Most of my travel these days is done two-up. While my girlfriend, Kristen has her license, she prefers riding on the back of my bike, especially for longer trips. There are some differences when traveling with a passenger as opposed to traveling by yourself.

Riding the Dragon two-up

One thing you'll want to do when planning your trip is seek input from your passenger on where they would like to visit and things they would like to see. Fortunately, Kristen and I agree on most things we want to see when it comes to our trips. I plan most of the route with the key highlight items, and she enjoys finding cool restaurants and lesser known things to check out along the way. It may work different with your passenger or they may not want to have any input into the trip. Even if they don't, it still good to offer up the opportunity to help plan.

When planning your trip, you'll definitely need to take your passenger into consideration when planning your route. While you may be able to handle 400 mile days, they may only be able to handle 300 miles per day. In some cases, it may be hard to determine how far they can ride comfortably on back-to-back days but it's better to ride a few less miles than too many.

If there is one negative to traveling with a passenger it's that you're going to have to share your storage space. In most cases the amount of luggage you can take will be cut in half or possibly even more. If you follow my "Rule of Five" detailed in Chapter 6, you should be fine.

It's possible that traveling with a passenger could defer some costs if they are paying for their half of the trip. You may be able to split things like hotel costs and fuel costs. This is definitely something you should discuss before taking the trip to ensure you're both on the same page.

Group

Traveling with a group or even one other rider can be a lot of fun, but it can also be a hassle. While it may be possible to plan the trip yourself and then just tell your buddies to follow along, in most cases it won't work out that way. They are going to want some sort of input on the trip.

I can tell you that I can cover far more miles in a day riding solo than I can riding in a group. Unless you're riding with a group of like-minded type riders, in most cases you'll be spending a few extra minutes at the fueling station, a few extra minutes trying to leave in the morning, a few extra minutes at lunch, etc. Those few extra minutes can add up to an hour or more throughout the day. Be sure to take into account the number of riders in your group and plan your daily mileage accordingly.

One advantage of riding with a group of riders is you should be able to save a little money on your trip. As long as you don't mind doubling up in a bed, you can fit four riders into a hotel room and split the cost four ways. Even if you want your own bed, you can still split the hotel room cost in half which will save you a significant amount of money on a multi-day trip.

Probably the biggest advantage of traveling with a group is you get to spend more time with your friends. Aside from the time you spend on your bike, there's just something special about riding to and discovering new places with your buddies. I've been fortunate enough to travel with family and friends on multiple occasions from overnighters to four and five day trips. I may have gotten a little irritated when we got off schedule and arrived after dark into a town, but they were also some of the best trips I've ever taken.

Budget

If you have unlimited funds, you can proceed to the next section. However, if you're like most people, your money is limited and must be allocated reasonably. We need to take some time to talk about budgeting for a trip. I'm not going to tell you how much to spend on your trip, but I will give you some suggestions on things you'll need to factor into your budget. Once you have that figure, you'll be able to make changes and tweaks to make sure you stay within budget to have a great trip but also one you can afford.

For short trips, I don't often figure out a budget. I have a very good idea of how much a two-night, three-day trip is going to cost, because I check the hotel costs ahead of time, have an idea of what food will cost and also have an educated guess on fuel. On longer trips, however, there are more variables to take into account.

Fuel will have to be factored into your budget. Luckily for motorcycle riders, fuel isn't as big of a line item as it would be for most automobiles or an RV. Hotels will likely be the biggest cost of your trip. I don't tend to stay in luxury hotels on my trips. I like to stay in clean, comfortable and affordable places. Best Westerns, Hampton Inns and Holiday Inn Expresses are some hotels I regularly book. Your next largest cost will likely be food. I don't usually spend a lot of money on breakfasts or lunches. I'll have the free breakfast at the hotel, though I'll typically eat breakfast at a restaurant every few days when I get tired of the hotel fare. Lunch is usually something fairly quick. I don't each much fast food, but I will eat something light for lunch. Dinner is where I spend the bulk of my dining money. Most nights, I don't go overboard. On a one to two-week trip I'll splurge on an expensive meal on one of the nights. I don't spend a lot of money on souvenirs, but that is something you'll want to remember to plan for in your budget.

There are two things many riders don't factor into their planning or budget. The first is an emergency fund. An emergency fund is a worst-case-scenario fund. Hopefully, you never have to use your emergency fund, but it's nice to know you have one. It's tough to say how much money you should have set aside should an emergency occur. I would consider emergencies to be breakdowns, crashes, injuries, and severe weather. In this context, it's really anything that's going to add significant cost or a significant delay in your trip. Having access to an extra $500 is a good starting point.

The other item many riders don't consider when taking a trip is the cost of maintenance after the trip. Things like oil changes, valve inspections, and new tires will creep up much faster when you're knocking out several back-to-back days at several hundred miles per day. If you do your own maintenance, the cost won't impact you nearly as much as relying on a mechanic or dealer. I don't say this to scare you out of taking a trip. I just want to point out that it's something to consider and budget accordingly.

Time of Year

When planning your trip, especially a longer trip, you will need to factor in the time of year you're planning to travel.

Early Spring

When the warm spring weather rolls in, all motorcyclists are excited to get on the road and enjoy the warmer temperatures. However, when it comes to motorcycle touring, you need to proceed with caution in early spring. The farther north you plan to travel, the longer the winter lasts. While it may be average highs in the mid-70s where you live, it's possible that 200-300 miles north of you that the highs may only reach the mid-40s or perhaps there is still snow on the ground in higher elevations.

In early spring, the highs don't last as long as they do in the summer, and the temperature changes are much more severe. The weather may be calling for a high of 65 degrees, but that may only be from 1:00-3:00 in the afternoon and by 5:00pm it's back down into the mid-50s. It's also possible that some parks and other areas may not be open due to the season, so be sure to check before booking hotels or making too many arrangements.

I've taken some great trips in the early spring. You just need to plan accordingly and make sure you have the right riding gear and know what type of weather to expect in the places you plan to travel.

Late Fall

Late fall can be a tricky travel time for many of the same reasons as early spring. I've been fortunate enough to do a few trips even as late as the middle of November, but you have to be cautious. The weather in the latter part of fall can change quickly. You could be experiencing summer-like temperatures one week and have snow the next. Kristen and I rode over Teton Pass in early September, and it was in the mid-70s when we arrived in Jackson Hole, WY. I saw on the news that less than two weeks after our trip through Teton Pass, they had snow. The weather can change that quickly.

I usually keep trips in the late fall much shorter than the ones I do in the summer. If you live in the southern part of the country, you can extend your riding season much longer than riders in more northern areas.

Holidays

Holidays are great because you don't have to work but it can also mean more traffic on the road, especially if that holiday makes for a three-day weekend. For the past few years, I've traveled on most holiday weekends like Memorial Day, Labor Day and Independence Day when it happens to make for a three-day weekend. I do have a few tips, observances and words of caution when it comes to traveling during the holidays.

It varies year to year, but in most cases the cost of fuel goes up right before a holiday weekend. Since we're riding motorcycles, it won't affect us much so I don't worry about it. Hotels are a price factor for a holiday weekend. Depending on where you're planning to visit, you may see no change in hotel prices. If you're planning to travel to the beach (more on that later), you could see room prices jump to more than double the usual price.

Speaking of the beach, I've found through the years that the closer you are to the coast on a holiday weekend, the more traffic you can expect. On a few occasions, I've ridden up or down the eastern seaboard on a holiday weekend, and every time I've experienced high volume traffic and plentiful delays. However, when traveling on those same holiday weekends to more inland states such as Ohio, Kentucky, Tennessee, and western Pennsylvania, I haven't experienced any influx of traffic though you may run into some larger crowds at touristy type stops.

Another way to battle the traffic on holiday weekends is to pull out your atlas and scout out some fun "motorcycle roads." Most holiday travelers will be taking interstates and major freeways to get to their destinations as quickly as possible. Seasoned motorcyclists know that in many cases the ride is more fun that the destination, so why not enjoy it on the best roads possible. Even if you get stuck behind a slow poke on a two-lane road, it's easy to twist your right wrist and get around them. So don't be deterred when it comes to traveling over holiday weekends, just make sure to keep some of these tips in mind.

Gather Your Supplies

Hopefully you gathered your supplies back at the beginning of the chapter, but if you haven't, now is the time. The following is what you're going to need and why you'll need it.

Notebook - Sure there are apps on your smartphone you could use that will serve the same purpose as a notebook. If that suits you better, by all means use them. I love technology, but I'm still old school when it comes to taking notes and the notebook reigns supreme.

Pencil - You'll need something to write down your ideas. I usually recommend a pencil because it has an eraser, and you're inevitably going to make mistakes and changes along the way. A pen will work fine as well as long as you don't mind scratching things out.

Computer/Tablet - Your computer or tablet are going to be invaluable when it comes to doing research for your trip. You can research almost anything with your computer including mileage, routes, hotels, restaurants, weather, etc. In a pinch, you could use your smartphone, but I prefer the bigger screen of a computer or tablet.

Atlas - I don't care what anyone says, there's nothing better for planning a trip than an atlas. Go to your local Walmart or truck stop and pick up a Rand McNally atlas. They're dirt cheap and worth their weight in gold to a traveler.

Notes/Ideas - I'm hoping you have some travel ideas or destinations already written down or documented. Get them ready because you're going to need them to help you form your trip.

Friends/Traveling Companions - If you're traveling with others, you need to make sure they're available. Even if they're going to allow you to plan the whole trip, you may still need to ask their opinion about certain things. They don't necessarily need to be there with you during the whole planning phase, but you should make sure they're available for input as you need it.

Planning

Drafts

You're probably going to go through multiple 'drafts' of your trip before deciding on a final plan. The longer the trip, the more drafts you'll go through before settling on your final trip plans. I've even gone through multiple drafts for overnight trips. The point is, don't get discouraged when you have to go back and change your route, it's going to happen often.

Using Notes

Most of my travel ideas and notes are written down in a notebook. Because I don't always carry my notebook, sometimes when I come across an idea I'll write it down on a post-it note, napkin, receipt, or loose sheet of paper. Sometimes I transcribe those notes into my notebook, but most of the time they just get tucked in between the pages. I use these notes and ideas to help me plan my trip. If you haven't been keeping a notebook of ideas, get a sheet of paper and write down any places you'd like to visit on your trip. As you come up with more ideas, write them down.

As I discussed earlier in the book, I also use Google Maps to track locations I'd like to visit. Have a tab in your web browser open with the Google Maps you've created so you can toggle back and forth. Also, gather any digital notes, screenshots, brochures, and other materials with travel ideas you may have collected.

Taking the time to gather and compile travel ideas throughout the year will make planning your trip much less difficult and less time consuming. In most cases, once I write down a place I'd like to visit, I begin to research it more thoroughly and write down some additional notes or details that may be important to consider when planning my trip. If you only have a rough idea of where you'd like to go, that's ok. It may take you a little longer, but I'm still going to show you how to plan out your motorcycle trip.

Google Maps

If you don't like using Google Maps and prefer to use MapQuest, Apple Maps or some other service, feel free to do so. Using Google Maps is a great way to get some rough estimates when you first begin planning your trip. Begin by entering your starting location for the day and your projected ending location. Because Google Maps will only allow you to toggle between the fastest route or the shortest route, the total mileage and time should only be a looked at as a rough estimate. In most cases, Google is going to choose routes which have a lot of interstates and highways. We'll get into how to customize the route later, but for now we just want a rough idea.

With your notebook handy, write down the starting point, ending point, estimated mileage and estimated time for each location you plan to stop on your trip. Below is an example of how one of my lists may look for the first day.

Start	End	Mileage	Time
Winchester, VA	Davis, WV	100	1:48
Davis, WV	Morgantown, WV	61	1:40
Morgantown, WV	St. Clairsville, OH	89	1:27
	Total	250	Approx. 5 hrs

Again, these are to be used as estimates. A more precise route will be assembled next. These figures are done to let you know if you're in the ballpark before spending too much time on the next step. If your estimated time is showing 10 hours for the day but you only wanted to ride for 7 hours, these estimates will show you the discrepancy early on in the planning process to allow you to make the necessary changes quickly and easily. If your mileage and time estimates are your desired range, it's now time to start coming up with a more precise route.

Atlas

GPS devices have come a long way over the years, but I still buy a new Rand McNally Road Atlas every year. Loaded with detailed maps, mileage charts, tourism information, interstate exit numbers, points of interest and much more, it's probably the best $20 a traveler can spend. One of the main reasons I like using an atlas to help plan my trips and routes is because it shows much more detail than any computer or GPS device. As you zoom out on most GPS devices, you lose detail. You don't have to worry about detail when using an atlas.

Using your atlas, look for roads you think you want to travel because they look like fun. For most motorcyclists, that means seeking out roads with lots of curves. Picking out a route is a lot like playing connect the dots. You're choosing different routes and roads to connect many small towns with the end goal of getting to your destination. Once you think you have a pretty good idea of the route you want to travel, go back to Google Maps and modify the route. Google Maps will allow you to click and drag the 'blue line' onto the exact road or roads you want. If you're greatly varying your route, you may have to add in additional 'stops' (towns) in order to get Google to route your map properly. Once again, write down the starting point, ending point, estimated mileage and estimated time. Additionally, you'll also want to write down a brief description of your route. Below is my updated example after choosing a specific route.

Start	End	Mileage	Time
Winchester, VA	Davis, WV	98	1:50
Rt50, Back Mountain Rd, Rt48			
Davis, WV	Morgantown, WV	71	1:42
Rt32, 219N, 24N, 50W, 92N, 119N			
Morgantown, WV	St. Clairsville, OH	91	2:22
19N, 7E, 250N, I470W			
	Total	260	Approx. 6 hrs

As you can see from this example, the mileage increased only 10 miles but the new route added approximately one hour of ride time. With the new total mileage number, you can safely figure you'll probably travel an extra 5-10% more miles. In the case of the previous example, you can expect to ride about 13-26 more miles than the total listed. The 5-10% increase factors in things like exit ramps, fuel stops, food stops, rest stops, scenic overlooks and pulling off to check out your points of interest.

Importance of an Atlas

I own a motorcycle-specific GPS, a smartphone and tablet with multiple GPS apps installed, and computer with access to Google Maps and other GPS sites. I've had great success using all of them, and I use a combination of them all to help me plan my routes for my trips. However, I still believe my $20 atlas is the most valuable trip planning tool I have at my disposal.

Many people have become so dependent on GPS and technology to get them places that they are unfamiliar with basic directions and are unable to navigate without a little computer telling them where to turn. If traveling via an interstate, you should know things like odd numbered interstates run north and south while the even numbered ones run east and west. Before you can take full advantage of your atlas, you need to understand how to read it. Be sure to check the legend to find out what all of the symbols and markings mean. Most people are surprised at the amount of detail that's included in a quality atlas once they understand how to read the information.

An atlas not only shows you where you are but also what's around you. It can show you how to get places and what's nearby your route along the way. I like to take my time and study my atlas, especially in the areas I'm planning to travel. Sometimes I'll find something while studying the atlas that piques my interest that is then added to my trip or added to my notebook as an idea for another trip. Even though I use a Garmin GPS on my trips, I don't need it. I commit my entire route to memory before I leave and then take a quick look at the atlas each morning while I'm on the trip to refresh my memory.

If you truly study your atlas, you'll be better prepared when things go awry. Ride enough miles and eventually you're going to run into a road closure, accident, traffic, construction or some sort of other delay. I've run into my fair share of construction or miscellaneous delays while traveling. Because I've taken the time to study the atlas for the majority of those situations, I've been able to modify my route to prevent further delays.

Atlases have a few other advantages over their more technological brethren. An atlas needs no batteries and is damn near impossible to break. Your atlas will also never get mad at you when you get off course. My Garmin and Siri on my iPhone both become irate even when I'm just hopping off an exit to get gas.

Give the atlas a chance before you label it too old school or if you're intimidated because you don't know how to read one. If you spend some time learning how to read and use an atlas, I think you'll find it very valuable and informative. Worst case scenario you'll be out $20, but I think you'll find the value much more than the price.

Estimating Travel Time

Using the method discussed earlier, your chart has provided you with an estimated amount of time you'll spend in the saddle. However, that's much different than total travel time. To figure out your total travel time, you're going to have to factor in stops. In my previous example, I knew I was going to stop in Davis, WV to see Blackwater Falls and then a stop in Morgantown, WV for lunch. If I were to leave at Winchester at 8:00am, I could safely presume I'd be in Davis by 10:00am, spend 30 minutes at the falls, and then get back on the road. From Davis to Morgantown should take me about an hour and 45 minutes which should put me in Morgantown around 12:15pm for lunch. I figured I'll spend about an hour in Morgantown getting lunch before getting back on the road (1:15pm) to get to my final destination of St. Clairsville, OH. With about two and a half hours left to ride, that should put me in St. Clairsville at approximately 3:45pm making my total travel time for the day just short of 8 hours.

I don't put much emphasis on factoring in fuel stops, rest stops or bathroom breaks. Unless you or your group take an inordinate amount of time checking phones, shooting the breeze or just generally wasting time during these stops, they really shouldn't have much impact on your travel time. In my example, I factored in time for lunch but I didn't do that on every day of the trip. On some days, I may just stop 15 minutes to get a sandwich and something to drink. Stops at points of interests are the ones that really need to be factored into your estimates.

In order to figure out how long you may spend at a point of interest, you're going to have to do some research. If you're planning to take a guided tour, most websites will list the tour length giving you a pretty good idea of how long it will take. Websites like TripAdvisor and Yelp provide dozens of detailed reviews from guests and visitors who many times can provide you with valuable information to assist in your planning. They'll post about things like wait times, which tours are best, things you must see, etc. One of the best things to do is talk to someone who's been there. If you have a friend or family member who has visited a place you're planning to visit, ask them about their experience. Most people will be more than happy to talk about their vacations and give you some good tips.

There are other places you may stop along that way that are just for a quick picture. I like planning for those types of stops because they make for great picture opportunities. I treat stops the same way I treat fuel stops in that I don't worry about factoring them into my travel time. With that said, do your research. You may find that some of the types of stops will require more time than you had anticipated. While it only takes a few seconds to snap a quick pic in front of the "Welcome to Fabulous Las Vegas Nevada" sign, the line can get very long and you can easily spend up to an hour waiting to take your picture. Taking the time to do your research ahead of time can make for more accurate estimations.

One last thing to keep in mind when estimating your travel time: it's only an estimation. A motorcycle trip should be fun, so unless you're one of those anal retentive types, don't treat it as a schedule. Your travel time estimations should only serve as a guideline to help you plan your trip.

Additional Research

The following are a few other items you'll want to pay particular attention to when planning your trip.

Hours of Operation - Most places will have standard hours of operation. However, you're likely to run into a handful of places when planning your trip that will have either oddball hours or varying hours. It's important to factor in a point of interest's operation hours when planning your trip. Be sure to give yourself enough time to check the place out without feeling rushed.

Days/Dates - Tourist destinations are likely to be open most days of the week, but the same may not be said for some places you may be planning to visit. For instance, I know of a smaller mom and pop store that's open every day of the week but Tuesday. With a couple minutes of research online, you should be able to find out a business or point of interest's days and hours of operation. If you're having trouble, in most cases you can pick up the phone and call. Also, be sure to double check operating status for holidays. Some places may be closed or alter their hours in observance of a holiday.

Season - Some places you plan to visit may be seasonal attractions. Kristen and I once rode across a covered bridge expecting to be able to tour the Old Bedford Village, only to find out it wasn't going to open for another month. Fortunately, it was just a stop along the way and not the whole reason for our trip.

Time - You need to do some research to figure out how much time you're going to spend at each stop. If people are saying you'll want to spend at least two hours in order to get the full experience, you don't want to be showing up an hour before closing.

Tickets - Some things you may want to do on your trip may require a ticket. In some cases, you may be able to buy a ticket once you arrive, while in others you may need to buy a ticket in advance. Be sure to do your research so you know what to expect before you arrive.

Where to Stop for the Night

For my first few trips, I would ride until I was ready to stop for the day, pull into a town and attempt to find a hotel. Sometimes that worked out well, while other times I would find out everything was booked and be forced to ride another hour to the next town to find a vacancy. On one particular trip we arrived in Waterbury, VT at dusk to find out there were no vacancies. We had to ride another 30 miles to Burlington in the dark as the temperature plummeted. Once we arrived in Burlington, it still took us a couple of stops before we found a hotel with two available rooms. I think it took my buddy Brad a couple of hours to thaw out as well.

When you're picking out a town to stop in for the night, it's important to take into account the number and type of accommodations they have available. It's also important to know how far away the next town of decent size is. I prefer to stay in an area that has at least a handful of different hotel and dining options. A quick Google search will show you what's around and in the area you plan to stop. The reason I mention the next town is because if you don't have a hotel reservation it's possible you may have to ride to the next town in order to find a place to stay.

Hotel Booking

Let's examine the different schools of thought on bookings hotels. I don't believe there is a right or a wrong way to go about booking your hotel room, and I've used all three methods over the years. While I mainly subscribe to one of the methods now, there's no guarantee that won't change in the future. I also want to share with you some tips to help pick out a great hotel for the night.

Booking Ahead of Time

Booking your hotel room ahead of time will ensure you have a room available when you arrive in town. In many cases, booking in advance will also get you a lower room rate. If there is a big event being held nearby or you're planning to stay in a popular tourist destination during their peak season, you may have no choice but to book a room weeks or even months in advance. If you're planning to book in advance, be sure to take special note of the terms and conditions. Find out what the cancellation policy is of the hotel. Many hotels will let you cancel your reservation up to 24 hours before check-in, but that policy isn't universal. Some hotels may have a two, four or even seven-day cancellation policy. Also, keep in mind you'll need to keep track of each hotel's policies you're planning to stay on your trip, as they are likely not all going to be the same. I've made reservations for hotels before that will give you a "no cancellation" rate, meaning you'll get a very low cost on the room but forfeit the right to cancel the reservation

Booking your room ahead of time can be great if everything works out as planned. If one thing knocks you off of your schedule, it can create a domino effect. Since we're riding motorcycles, weather is normally one of the biggest culprits in ruining even the best of plans. I've had a handful of trips get changed due to weather. I didn't have any reservations made ahead of time, but if I had, it would've meant calling multiple hotels to cancel and/or reschedule reservations.

I seldom book things in advance, because I don't like having to worry about cancellation policies or sticking to a tight schedule. I book in advance in two circumstances. 1) If it's an overnight trip, I may book the room a few days or up to a week in advance. If I do end up needing to cancel, I only have to make one call so it's not much of a pain. 2) If I'm planning to stay in an area where a big event is being held and rooms will be scarce, I'll reserve a room. I only need to cancel one reservation if something comes up.

Booking the Same Day

Booking the same day is the method I currently use most often. When I stop for lunch, I'll book my hotel for that day. By lunchtime, I know if I'm on pace to make it to my destination that afternoon or evening. By booking at lunch, I know my room will be reserved and available when I arrive. If I find out all the hotels in that area are booked, I can check another nearby town and alter my plans if need be.

There are a few reasons I prefer making a reservation the same day. I like knowing when I arrive into town later that day I will have a room available, and I'm not going to have to hunt around. Unlike booking far in advance, I don't have to worry about canceling a room because I'm only making the reservation a few hours in advance. The final thing I like about booking the same day is sometimes you get a special discounted price because they're trying to sell the last few rooms for the night. Sites like Hotels.com and Expedia.com will show you these "special" prices, sometimes allowing you to save as much as 50%.

Waiting Until You Arrive

Occasionally, I still wait until I roll into town before attempting to get a room for the night. Sometimes there aren't any rooms left by the time I arrive. There's no right or wrong way to book a hotel room, but if you're going to wait until you arrive in town you should always have a backup plan and know how far away the closest town is should you need to ride there to get a room. If you're friendly to the front desk person, sometimes they'll be nice enough to contact one of their partner hotels on your behalf to check availability and reserve you a room.

Choosing a Hotel

Hampton Inn, Holiday Inn Express and other hotels similar in amenities and price are the types of hotels I prefer for my trips. We all have different budgets to work with and we all like different things, so it should come as no surprise that we aren't necessarily going to agree on what makes one hotel better than another. With that being said, I want to share with you a few tips to ensure you get the hotel room that suits you best.

Ratings/Reviews

Websites and apps such as Yelp, Hotels.com, and TripAdvisor have made it much easier to narrow down hotel choices. Don't just rely on the star ratings. Take a few minutes to read through a handful of reviews. Some reviews don't have much information at all, some are just written by generally unhappy people, and then others will provide a well thought out and informative review that's either positive, negative or neutral. Also, keep in mind what some people may think is a positive, you may find as a negative or vice-versa. I've read a few reviews where people were upset about something like the pool not being heated. I didn't view that as a positive or negative, as it didn't affect me at all.

Ratings and reviews are just one metric I use when picking out a hotel. As I discussed earlier, budget is also a concern.

Price

The Ritz Carlton may have glowing reviews and a 5-star rating, but if I'm not prepared to drop $300 a night it's not going to make the cut. My choice of hotel isn't exact science. If two hotels are seemingly seen as equal in the reviews and ratings and one is $50 less than the other, I'm probably going to go with the cheaper option and put that $50 toward dinner.

Price can also be used as a discriminating factor even before checking out the reviews. If something is far out of your price range, it doesn't make sense to waste time reading about it. Most booking apps and websites will let you filter hotels by price, so setting a price ceiling may be a good way to eliminate some of the options that are too expensive or even too cheap for your taste.

Location

Location is the final determining factor I use to choose a hotel. After reading a few reviews and checking the pricing to find hotels in my budget, I'm normally able to narrow my choices down to a few places. I like staying at hotels that are within walking distance of a restaurant or handful of restaurants, so once I'm at the hotel I can leave the bike parked for the night. If it's laundry night, I may also be looking for a hotel that's near a laundromat.

It's actually quite easy to find out what's right around the hotel. I grab the hotel's address from their website or booking app and enter it into my smartphone GPS. With the hotel's location loaded into my phone, I can zoom in and out on my Maps app which will show surrounding restaurants, shopping and other businesses. You're likely to find that all of the hotels are within a few hundred yards of each other and in equally desirable locations.

Final Word on Planning

I hope this chapter has given you plenty of food for thought but more importantly tools you can use to plan your trip. Planning a trip isn't a linear process. You're going to make all sorts of mistakes along the way. Making mistakes is how you learn. Planning a trip is a skill and the more you do it the better you'll get. My planning process has been developed through a lot of trial and error as well as consulting those who are much more experienced at it than me. Don't feel like you have to use the same methods and steps to plan your trips as I use to plan mine. Pick and choose the methods, tools and tips that works best for you.

Chapter 6
Final Preparation

You have your trip planned, and now it's time to get down to the final preparation. I'm going to break preparation down into three main sections. The first section will cover preparations that need to be done to your bike. The second section will include things you'll need to pack, and the third section will cover other miscellaneous items you may need to plan ahead of time.

The Bike

While I prefer to work on my own machine, you may have most of the following performed or checked by your dealer or mechanic. I would suggest doing as much of the preparation and checking of your bike as possible. The better familiarity and understanding you have of your motorcycle, the better equipped you'll be to handle any problems you may experience while on your trip.

Clean Your Bike

Cleaning your bike is one of the simplest things you can do to keep your bike running well. Your paint will last longer and stay looking bright if it's clean and waxed on a regular basis. However, there are other reasons to keep your bike clean. With a clean bike, you'll be more likely to spot leaks before they become a bigger problem. You may also spot frayed wires or cracked brake lines before they can cause a serious issue. Brake dust can do damage to painted surfaces, so it's best to keep those painted wheels clean. I've seen bikes get so much brake dust built up that it can interfere with the brake calipers function and make it very difficult to remove when replacing the pads. Cleaning your bike doesn't always mean washing it. In some cases, I've used some spray cleaner and a couple of microfiber towels to give it a good polish.

Maintenance

My dad has always said, "Take care of your machine and it will take care of you." Keeping up on the routine maintenance of your bike will keep it running great. Before any trip, be it an overnighter or even longer, you need to go over your bike to ensure it's in proper order. While specifics will vary from model to model, you should be looking for the same things on all bikes. Make sure the tires are free of punctures and properly inflated; check to make sure there are no leaks; ensure there are no loose fasteners; make sure the suspension is working properly; if equipped with a chain, make sure it's in proper adjustment.. Most owner's manuals will provide you with a list of items you should check before each ride, and I highly recommend heeding their advice.

When it comes to preparing for a trip, you'll need to take into account your next scheduled maintenance interval. Trips under 1,000 miles may not make much difference, but if you're planning a 2,500 mile trip you need to pay close attention to your owner's manual to make sure you don't significantly go past an upcoming maintenance item. For instance, if your spark plugs are due to be replaced in 1,000 miles but you're planning a 3,000 mile trip, you may want to change them before you leave. On the flip side, maybe your next oil change is supposed to be in 3,500 miles and you're planning to go on a 3,700 mile trip. In this case, you may elect to wait until you get back to change the oil.

When planning your next trip, be sure to check your owner's manual and maintenance records. Compare the next maintenance interval to the mileage of your upcoming trip to see which, if any, maintenance item will be due. Some may decide to take their bike to the dealer to have all the maintenance done a little earlier while others, like me, will decide what work needs to be done now and what can wait until after we get back. Either way you decide to tackle it will ensure your bike is in top running order.

Tires

Tires are often forgotten. Much like the scheduled maintenance, a tire's life needs to be taken into account before heading off on a long motorcycle trip. Tire wear is never an exact science, but you should have a good idea of how long your tires will last. If your rear tire currently has 3,000 miles on it and looks about half worn, I wouldn't take a 3,500 mile trip before putting on a fresh tire. In 2015, I pulled a set of tires off of my bike that had 4,000 miles of tread left on them. I was getting ready to take off on a trip that totaled about 4,700 miles, so there was no way I was going to make it on that set. After I eventually wore out the next set (which didn't take me long), I put the set back on that had 4,000 miles of life left. There was absolutely nothing wrong with the worn tires; they just weren't going to make the trip to the Grand Canyon and back. I have access to my own tire changing equipment, so it costs me nothing to change tires. I know many readers will need to pay a dealer or tire shop to change their tires which can get pricy. If it doesn't make financial sense to put a used tire back on you, may still be able to recoup some of your loss by selling the tire to a buddy or listing it on a site like Craigslist. In any event, be sure your tires will make it to the end of your trip or replace them before you leave. If in doubt, error on the side of caution and replace them earlier rather than later.

One more thing when it comes to tires. Make sure you scrub, or break in, in your new tires before you leave on a trip. The best way to scrub your new tires is to get them up to a safe operating temperature. You may have noticed new tires are really slippery when you get them. By getting the tires up to operating temperature, the heat will help to leech out all the oils or chemicals in the tire that will make it slick. Break in your new tires by putting them through some strong acceleration and braking while upright to generate heat in the tire carcass. Once the tires have some heat in them, I'd recommend hitting up one of your favorite winding roads to further break them in and make sure they are working well. Scrubbing in your new tires before you leave does three things: 1) Helps remove the slick chemicals from the tires' surface 2) Allows you to check the tires are properly balanced and working correctly 3) Allows the tire to firmly seat on the rim. Be sure to check the tire pressure again when the tire is cold. Many times, I'll find the psi has dropped a pound or two after the first ride.

Upgrades and Modifications

The following items are suggestions of things you may want to buy or do to your motorcycle in preparation for a long-distance trip. Please don't view this as a checklist of things you need to buy or have. Some motorcycles will come from the factory with many of the things I have listed, while others may be dealer options or aftermarket add-ons. While most of these items you don't need, I wanted to make you aware of them so you can set your bike up to make it the best for you and your riding style.

Luggage

When it comes to luggage, there are many different products and combinations of products that can be used on motorcycles. I'm going to attempt to cover most of them to give you an idea of what's available.

Hard Saddlebags

Most touring and sport touring motorcycles will come from the factory with hard saddlebags. However, just because your bike didn't come with them doesn't mean you can't get them. Some manufacturers will offer them as a dealer option or add on, while aftermarket manufacturers will make hard saddlebags to fit almost any bike. In some factory or dealer option cases and in almost all aftermarket cases, you're also going to need to buy a mounting and/or installation kit in order to mount hard saddlebags onto your motorcycle. Givi and Touratech, who make the factory bags for some makes and models, are two of the most recognizable names in aftermarket luggage, but there are many other great manufacturers worth checking out as well.

There are some serious benefits in having hard saddlebags. In most cases, they are waterproof allowing you to keep your luggage safe from the elements. Almost all hard saddlebags are also lockable, so you don't have to worry about your belongings walking away while you're away from your bike. Some of the heavier-duty ones, usually found on adventure bikes, can take a pretty good beating and keep your stuff safe in case of a crash as well.

While many riders love their hard saddlebags, some don't like them as much. For one thing, hard bags do add more weight to the bike. Many are rather large so they will add more wind drag to the bike as well. The one big negative to hard saddlebags is the price. Aftermarket saddlebags plus the cost of the mounting kit and/or brackets can take the cost up over $1,000 and in some cases more than $2,000.

If your bike didn't come with hard saddlebags, they are definitely something to consider. Just don't be shocked by the price. One last tip on hard saddlebags: if available, be sure to purchase the bag liners. Bag liners are like soft suitcases that are custom made to fit inside the bags. When packing, if it fits in the liner, it'll fit in the saddlebag. The other great thing is you can just carry the liner in your hotel room at night and leave the saddlebag locked on the bike.

Top Case

A top case, sometimes called a trunk, is another piece of hard luggage available from the factory or as a dealer option. Top cases are also available from many aftermarket companies as well. As with hard saddlebags, top cases are waterproof and lockable providing a safe way to protect your belongings from the elements and unsavory characters. While they come in different sizes, some are built large enough to hold a full-face helmet or two. Another great thing about top cases is if you travel two-up, it can provide your passenger with a backrest. Some top cases even have the option to add on a padded backrest to make your passenger even more comfortable. Some can make your bike more visible to traffic by having auxiliary lights built into them that can add additional rear lighting, brake lighting and in some cases turn signals. Along with the top case, you'll likely need to purchase a mounting kit and/or bracket as well. Top cases with the mounting kit in most cases cost around half the price of a pair of saddlebags, so expect to pay around $500-$1000 for most.

Soft Saddlebags

Soft saddlebags are a more cost-effective alternative to hard bags. They can be purchased for much less and in some cases may not need additional mounting hardware. Soft bags are much lighter than hard bags which is another reason some riders prefer them. Some manufacturers offer waterproof soft saddlebags so you can keep your gear dry just like the hard bags. The downside is there is no way to safely lock the bags, as most can easily be removed from the bike or cut with a knife. In the event of a crash, soft bags will not protect your belongings as well as hard bags. As with the hard bags, there are pros and cons to each. I have traveled quite a bit with both types, and it comes down to a personal choice.

Tail Bag

A tail bag is a bag that goes on the back of the motorcycle. A tail bag is essentially just a travel bag with some motorcycle-specific mounting options, such as straps, hook and loop fastening or a combination. Some riders will use these in conjunction with some sort of saddlebags, while some may use the tail bag as their only piece of luggage. Tail bags are versatile and come in many different styles and sizes. Fortunately, they aren't very expensive with most models starting out under $100 and a few above the $300 mark.

Tank bag

The tank bag is probably the most owned piece of motorcycle-specific luggage for motorcyclists. It's the category of motorcycle luggage with the most choices as well. While recently browsing a large on-line motorcycle retailer's website, I saw they had over 150 different choices when it comes to tank bags.

I believe tanks bags are so popular because they provide the most convenient access to your belongings. In order to access your saddlebags, tail bag or top case, you need to get off of your motorcycle but you can access your tank bag from your seat. As with tail bags, tank bags come in all sorts of styles and sizes.

Every year, manufacturers are coming up with new features to add into tank bags.

Traditionally, tank bags are mounted by using magnets or straps. The ones with magnets built into them will attract to the metal gas tanks which can be found on most motorcycles. However, some bikes have plastic tanks or tanks made of other materials, so the tank bag can be strapped on in many cases using some sort of quick release buckles to attach it or take it off the bike without having to remove the entire strap.

I have always found two negatives with tank bags: 1) The amount of time it takes to remove and reinstall the bag at each fillup 2) They will inevitably scratch the paint on your tank. Fortunately, manufacturers have (for the most part) solved both of those problems. Companies are now making quick-release bags that lock onto the tank. These quick-release bags fix the first issue, because they only take a split second to take off the bike and split second to reinstall. Also, you don't have to worry about getting the bag perfectly realigned because it clicks right back into place in the exact location it belongs. They've also solved the problem with the bag scratching the tank because the bag no longer touches the tank. The quick-release bags clip onto a retaining ring that is mounted to the frame of your gas cap. The great thing about these bags is they will mount to a metal or plastic tank. If there is a downside, it's that you will need a separate retaining ring for each bike you plan to use this bag on as the retaining rings are motorcycle make and model specific.

Having used many different tank bags from many different manufacturers with many different mounting systems, I can safely say the quick-release bags are by far my favorite.

Windshields

Windshields do a great job of protecting riders from the elements. Not only can they keep the wind from beating you up all day, they can also keep you warmer when it gets cold outside by keeping the cold air from hitting you directly. Most new riders are surprised to find that a windshield can protect a rider pretty well from the rain or other precipitation as long as you're in motion. Another benefit windshields provide is protection from bugs and other debris. I've often looked at my bug-splattered windshield after a long day of riding and been thankful the windshield took the brunt of it and not me.

Most touring bikes come with a windshield or windscreen from the factory. Some of the windshields are adjustable. I've owned bikes with electronically adjustable windshields, manually adjustable windshields you can adjust on the fly and windshields you need tools to adjust. Many manufacturers offer additional dealer options when it comes to windshields. Aftermarket manufacturers have dozens of different options per bike when it comes to windshields. While you may have the same make and model bike as your friend, if he's 4 inches taller than you, there's a good chance you'll prefer different windshields. Riders who travel back roads in warmer climates will likely prefer a shorter windshield than riders who do lots of interstate riding in cooler climates. Rider height, riding style, climate and personal preference are all important factors in finding the windshield that works best for your bike.

Not all motorcycles come with a windshield from the factory, but fear not, there is an excellent chance an aftermarket company makes a windshield for your bike. Cruisers have an almost unlimited selection of windshield choices. Some come with a quick-release mounting bracket, so if you want to take a quick ride and feel the wind in your face you can quickly remove the windshield and then easily put in back on when you get home. Standard motorcycles have quite a few choices as well when it comes to aftermarket windshields. Sportbikes usually only have about 2-3 choices per model. While they aren't going to punch as big of hole in the air as the windshields on touring bikes, they can make a huge improvement over the factory screen. Dualsport riders are going to face the most difficulty in finding an aftermarket windshield. There are very few made commercially, but I have seen pretty creative guys on some of the dirt bike forums.

If you don't have a windshield on your bike, I recommend looking into one before taking off on a motorcycle trip. I think you'll find it a very worthwhile investment.

Headsets

While most headsets these days don't necessarily go on your bike, I believe this section is the best place to talk about them. If you're traveling with a group of people or just a passenger, a headset can make communicating much easier and much more convenient. While older systems still exist, almost all manufacturers and riders have moved over to Bluetooth headsets. Bluetooth headsets are battery powered and can be mounted directly within the helmet. In addition to allowing you to speak to other riders or passengers, they will also allow you to make phone calls, listen to music and get turn-by-turn directions. I've had one for the last few riding seasons and love it. I would suggest looking at Sena or Scala brands to start. Expect to pay around $200 for a quality headset.

Cruise Control (or something like that)

While cruise control is starting to come standard on more motorcycles, it's still the exception rather than the rule. I just recently purchased my first bike with cruise control. I will admit that it's nice, but just because you don't have cruise control doesn't mean you can't do a cross-country trip. At this point, I've still taken my longest rides on bikes without cruise control, including my Iron Butt ride. (An Iron Butt Saddle Sore 1000 is a 1,000 motorcycle ride in under 24 hours.)

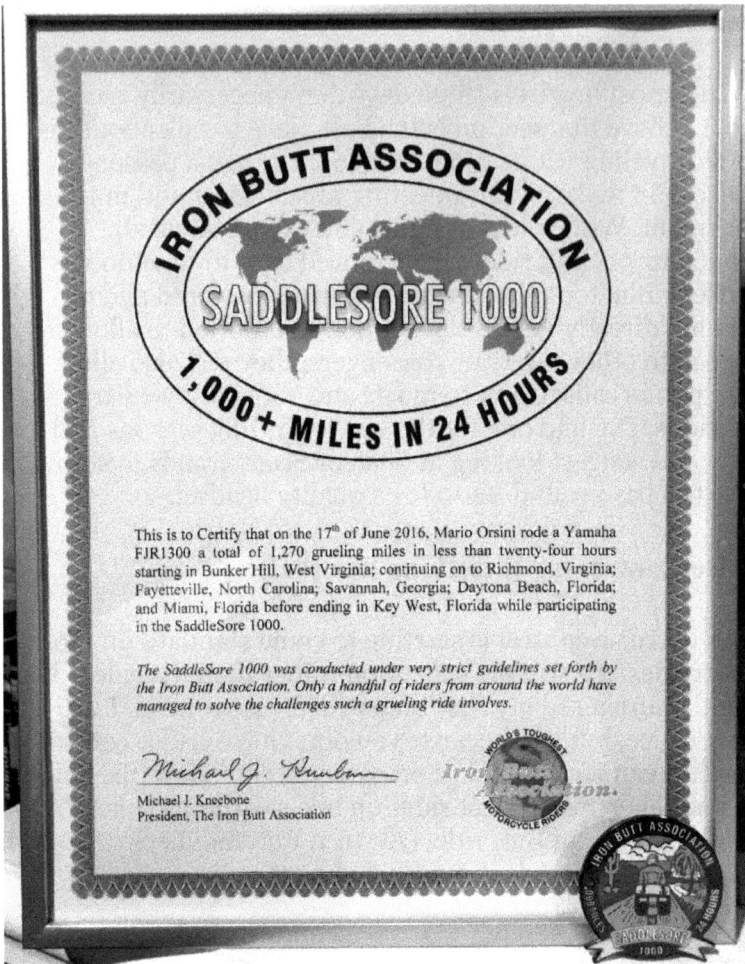

Iron Butt Association Certificate

There are quite a few different devices on the market that operate as throttle locks. A throttle lock is a device that "locks" your throttle in place allowing you to release the throttle of the motorcycle. Most throttle locks use friction on the end of the bar or some sort of mechanical device to hold the throttle in place. They can range in price from around $20 up to a few hundred dollars. Because the throttle lock "locks" your throttle in place, the spring will not snap it back when you let go. To close the throttle while the throttle lock is engaged, you'll have to either disengage the device or manually turn the throttle back to close. Please keep in mind, throttle locks are not a true cruise control so the speed of the bike will change fairly significantly with inclines or declines. I've known many riders who like using throttle locks. I've only had one bike with a throttle lock and seldom used it.

One device I really like using is the Crampbuster. The Crampbuster allows you to control your throttle with a relaxed hand. It's a very simple device that can be put on either end of your throttle grip using no tools. It can be installed or removed in a matter of seconds. Crampbuster is also adjustable on the fly. Even on a bike equipped with cruise control, I still use the Crampbuster. Because cruise control is really only good for long straight stretches, the Crampbuster comes in very handy on state routes and backroads. You can use it to stretch your hand a bit on a short straightaway before braking the bike again for the next corner entry. The product is so affordable, about $10, and I like it so much I've bought one for most of my friends and family members who ride. I've received nothing but positive feedback from all of them.

Highway Pegs

Highway pegs are excellent for longer rides, as they will allow you to stretch your legs without having to get off of the bike. Highway pegs are usually found on cruisers and touring bikes, however they can also be found from aftermarket companies for sport touring and adventure bikes. I suppose, if you got creative enough, highway pegs could be added to just about any bike. Expect to pay around $200 or more for a set of highway pegs. They can normally be installed on your bike in a matter of minutes with just some simple hand tools. If you want to make your bike more comfortable, add some highway pegs; your knees will thank you.

Seat/Seat Cover

The comfort of a motorcycle seat is a highly subjective topic which usually leads to some very strong opinions in forums and owners groups. I will say most cruiser, touring and sport touring bikes come with pretty good seats from the factory. Some manufacturers even offer some dealer option seats such as gel seats, comfort seats and even seats that will lower the overall seat height. Aftermarket companies also make seats for most of the popular makes and models. Many of these aftermarket seats range from $400 to well over $1,000 dollars. If you don't like your factory seat, dealer option seat choices or the aftermarket choices, you can have a custom seat made for your bike. Fees for custom seats can range from around $100 up to several hundred dollars for more. In most cases, your stock seat or seat pan is used as the base for your new custom seat. Custom seats are probably the best options for really tall riders.

If you'd like to make your seat more comfortable without spending a lot of money, a seat cover may be what you need. There are dozens of different seat covers available from beaded covers to inflatable ones. Personally, I've never felt the need to buy an aftermarket seat or try any sort of motorcycle-specific seat cover. I've always stuck with my tried and true sheepskin. A sheepskin can be purchased for under $100 and used for years. Not only does it provide some extra cushioning, but it also keeps your rear much cooler in warmer weather which is something most aftermarket seat and seat covers can not claim. I've converted some friends over to the sheepskin too, and they won't go back to anything else. Again, motorcycle seat comfort is highly subjective so go with the option that suits you best.

Bike Cover

The first overnight motorcycle trip I took, I didn't have a bike cover. On every other trip since then, I've brought my cover along. Bike covers can range from $30 to around $200 if you want a bike-specific cover with the make and/or model of the bike printed on it. A cover will serve you in several ways on a trip. The most obvious one is to keep the weather off the bike while it's parked. With no cover, even if it doesn't rain overnight, it's possible to come out to a bike with a wet seat from dew or frost. It can also be used on longer stops during the day at a point of interest or lunch to keep the sun from heating up your seat. I think the most important reason to use a bike cover is to keep people away from and off of your bike. You'd be surprised how powerful a simple piece of nylon can be at keeping your bike safe. I haven't seen anyone yet try to remove my cover (or any other rider's), but I have seen plenty touch and even sit on bikes that don't belong to them when they aren't covered.

When it comes to picking out a cover, you can get a motorcycle-specific cover or a generic cover. The motorcycle-specific covers are made to perfectly fit your model of bike. Some of these covers may have the manufacturer name or the model name printed on them as well. Motorcycle-specific covers are usually the most expensive. Generic covers usually have a size range and while they may not perfectly fit every piece of the bike, they still accomplish the same job. Think of generic and motorcycle-specific covers as off-the-rack vs. tailored suits; they both do the same job, one just looks a little better. Both of the above mentioned covers provide the maximum amount of coverage by covering the entire bike all the way down to the ground. One downside to full covers is they tend to be bulky and take a large amount of space on the bike. You also need to be careful and let the bike cool down before installing the cover, since the engine and exhaust pipes can get extremely hot.

I travel with a half cover. A half cover comes about halfway down on the bike usually leaving the front fender and wheel exposed. While it doesn't provide as much coverage or protection, I prefer it to a full cover. The half cover will still keep the seat dry or cool and keep anything in the dash or tank area out of view. It will also deter people just as much from getting on the bike as the full cover. Because it doesn't cover the engine or exhaust, I can put it on immediately without having to worry about it melting. The half cover also takes up far less space on the bike, and when you're traveling on a big trip space is at a premium. Mine takes up about as much room as a fanny pack.

If you decide to take a cover along while traveling, don't feel like you have to spend a lot of money. For as little as $30 you can keep sleep soundly at night knowing your bike is protected.

Power Outlet

Your bike may already have a power outlet, but if it doesn't you can always add one. Even if your bike does have a power outlet, it's possible to add another. Power outlets come in handy for charging your cell phone or other electronic devices while you're on your bike. They're also good for plugging in your heated riding gear should you be wearing any. If you have some basic wiring knowledge, you should have no problem hooking one up.

Another alternative to a power outlet is a USB plugin. While it's true you can get a USB plugin that will fit in a 12V power outlet, you can also get a dedicated USB plugin. I've used the one made by Battery Tender which is around $10 and takes only minutes to install. It connects directly to the battery using the familiar Battery Tender pigtail. Once installed, you can power or charge any USB device. Because it uses the same leads as all other Battery Tender devices, if you keep your leads on your battery year round, you can install it in seconds

GPS

A handful of bikes are available with GPS from the factory. For most bikes, you'll have to go to the aftermarket in order to find a GPS unit for your motorcycle. Motorcycle-specific GPS units are made to be weatherproof, meaning they can withstand a wide range of temperatures, water and even being dropped. Most GPS units for cars will not hold up like the motorcycle units. In addition to being built more rugged, they usually have different software installed on them as well. Some models will have software to help you plot points for off road enduring riding while others will provide you with "fun motorcycle routes" to ride from point to point. Motorcycle-specific GPS units are usually quite a bit more than their automobile counterparts. While most come with mounting equipment, you may have to buy additional brackets or hardware to get the best fit on your bike. You'll also need to wire the GPS to your bike unless you plan to use the built-in battery exclusively.

With smartphone advances the last few years, most riders will probably be content using the built-in GPS on their phone. Is a motorcycle-specific GPS worth the money? Again, it will come down to a personal choice. That said, if you can afford one, I don't think you'll regret the decision.

RAM Mounts

Round-A-Mount, or RAM Mounts for short, make some of the coolest and most versatile mounting devices for your motorcycle as well as other applications. RAM Mounts can be used to mount things like a GPS, smartphone, camera or even cup holder to your bike. They use a patented ball-and-socket design that will provide a secure hold from any road vibration. RAM mounts are a mix-and-match type of item that will allow you custom build a mount to your particular needs. Almost all RAM pieces are interchangeable with one another. They've made quite a reputation for themselves in the motorcycle community for their durability and usefulness. Having used them myself, RAM Mounts are invaluable. If you're looking for a mounting solution for your bike, I would start with RAM Mounts first. I don't think you'll be disappointed.

Tool Kit

Not long ago, all motorcycles came with a tool kit; that's not necessarily the case anymore. Even bikes that do come with a tool kit will sometimes leave out essential tools you may need in the case of an emergency on the road. If your bike didn't come with a tool kit (or even if it did), there are some great aftermarket tool kits available that include quality tools. Every tool kit should have allen and/or torx keys, screwdrivers, pliers, and an adjustable wrench and/or sockets.

In addition to those items, I would recommend adding a few additional things. Zip ties are invaluable and take up almost no space, so be sure to throw a handful of those into your kit. A small flashlight will not only help when it's dark but also when you need to see into some crevices of your bike. Gaffers tape, duct tape and electrical tape can be used for many different things. You can find small battery cables that can fit under the seat and get you a jump should you have a dead battery (or you could learn to bump start your bike). A very small can of WD40 and a bottle of Loctite could be added to your kit. Also, don't forget to carry a couple of extra fuses. Finally, a Leatherman tool, Swiss Army knife or just a regular pocket knife can be worth their weight in gold.

Every rider (or at least someone in your group) should have some sort of tire repair kit. There's nothing worse than a flat tire on your motorcycle, so being able to fix it alongside the road or at least patching it long enough to get you to the next town is essential. Some riders will carry tires irons, extra tubes and patch kits. Depending on the type of wheels and tires you have, that may be the best idea. I carry a tire plug kit and also a small air compressor. The air compressor can be plugged into a 12V outlet or you can attach the alligator clips directly to the battery to power it. Other kits will include an inflator that uses a CO_2 cartridge. Knock on wood, I've never had to use my kit on a trip, but I have used it to plug a couple of tires for friends and it works great. There are quite a few different repair kits available. Just make sure you're familiar with how it works before heading out on the road.

Packing

In this section, I'm going to provide my general guidelines for how I pack for a motorcycle trip. I realize you may have slightly different needs than me, so feel free to pick and choose the parts that work for you. Also, I'm going to list quite a few things to pack that may or may not apply to you and your trip. Again, feel free to use what works best for you.

Clothing

We're going to start with clothing since that will comprise the bulk of your luggage. Unless you're 100% certain of the weather, always prepare to dress in layers. On a motorcycle, you're exposed to the elements so the temperature in the afternoon may be very different than the temperature at eight o'clock in the morning. The following suggestions are making the assumption that you will be wearing some sort of riding gear meaning at least a helmet, jacket, gloves and boots.

Rule of Five

Before we get started in what clothing to pack let, me explain my Rule of Five. The Rule of Five is how I pack for a trip and it's really easy. If I'm traveling for five days or less, I pack enough clothing to last me for the number of days I'll be gone (with one exception that I'll explain later). For instance, if I'm traveling for three days, I pack enough clothing for three days. If I'm traveling for five days, I pack enough clothing for five days. However, using the Rule of Five, once I pass five or more travel days, I only pack enough clothing for five days. It doesn't matter if I'm planning on six travel days or fifteen travel days, I only pack enough clothing to last me five days.

You may wonder what I do once I run out of clothes. Well, that's actually pretty simple...laundry. On "laundry night," we find a hotel with a washer and dryer or try to stay near a laundromat and get our clothes cleaned. You can pack detergent if you like, but I normally just get some from the hotel or laundromat. Even though I referred to it as "laundry night," it takes less than two hours so it won't take up your entire evening. We usually use the time to get showers and figure out where we want to go to eat. By packing for five days, you can fit all of your clothes in just one saddlebag and leave plenty of room for souvenirs and other things.

Shirts

I'm presuming you are not wearing polos or button down shirts while touring on your motorcycle, so I'm going to speak mostly about t-shirts. Using the Rule of Five, you'll pack up to 4 t-shirts or the number of days your trip is going to last, whichever is less. You're only going to pack 4 t-shirts, because you're already wearing one. I would also recommend packing at least one long-sleeve t-shirt or sweatshirt to use for layering.

Pants

If you're wearing riding pants, I would only pack one additional pair of pants. In most cases, you can wear your riding pants day after day and get away with washing them once a week. I typically pack a pair of jeans or shorts depending on the weather of my destination. If you're riding in regular jeans, you can usually get 2-3 days out of a pair before they'll need to be washed (alternate jeans each day).

Underwear

Underwear follows the Rule of Five plus one. Always pack an EXTRA pair of underwear. Accidents can and do happen! While you may be able to get away with wearing some articles of clothing more than once, I don't want to try that with underwear and I doubt you will either.

Socks

Socks follow the Rule of Five. You may want to throw in a pair of low cut socks if you plan to bring sneakers along, but otherwise just pack four pairs of socks suitable to ride in and you should be fine.

Shoes

Most motorcycle-specific boots are not very comfortable for walking around off of the bike. I wear a very comfortable pair of touring boots while traveling that are actually pretty good for walking at different stops along the way. Some of you may just ride in a regular hiking boot which are obviously good for walking in as well. No matter if you wear a very technical riding boot or a comfortable hiking boot, I would recommend bringing another pair of shoes. I would however limit it to just ONE pair since they take up a lot of space on the bike.

I like to get my feet out of my boots once I'm done riding for the day. Depending on the length of the trip and the destination(s), I usually limit my choices in extra shoes to either sneakers or sandals. Since I wear a size 12, they take up a LOT of real estate on the bike, but I think it's worth it. I usually go with sandals if I'm going to really hot areas and sneakers for everywhere else. I like to pack a low-cut sneaker such as Chuck Taylors or low-cut training shoe. I have no room on my bike for high tops.

Ball Cap

Take a ball cap. Being a motorcyclist, I'm sure you take one with you most everywhere to avoid the dreaded "helmet hair." I know I do! If you're bald, still take a ball cap. It'll keep you from burning your head while you're checking stuff out off the bike. It'll also keep the sun out of your eyes.

Sunglasses

Speaking of sun, remember to take a pair of sunglasses. If you wear eyeglasses, be sure to take your prescription sunglasses or your clip-on sunglasses. Not only will they protect your eyes from the sun, they'll also keep you from having to squint in pictures.

Toiletries

I'm sure it's going to be different for everyone, but I pack, deodorant, toothpaste, toothbrush, sunscreen, and hair gel. If I'm only going to be gone a few days, I leave the razor at home. Sometimes I leave it at home on longer trips as well because most hotels will give you a razor and shaving cream if you request it. Almost all hotels will also provide you with soap, lotion, shampoo and conditioner in your room, so there's no need to pack any of that stuff either unless you require a specific kind. Yes, it's possible to get a free toothbrush and toothpaste as well, but I prefer to take my own.

Recently, I've been packing sunscreen and keeping it in my tank bag. Even with a dark tinted face shield, you'll still get plenty of sun on your face. Spend enough time on the bike and your face may burn, so I've started applying sunscreen to my face in the mornings and again at lunch if warranted. Be sure to use a sport-type formula that won't melt off your face when you start sweating. A sport formula will help keep your helmet liner from getting dirty and soiled. I'm sure there are other good reasons for using sunscreen, but keeping your skin from getting burned is a good enough reason for me.

If you need more toiletries than I travel with, check out the travel section of your local department store. They have all sorts of small travel-size bottles of toiletries. If you are unable to find what you need, you can buy empty bottles and fill them up. We've also used Ziploc bags to put things like laundry detergent in to save money and space. There are quite a few "travel hack" websites and YouTube videos you can check out for more ideas. My recommendation is to pack as little as possible. You can (almost) always buy what you need on the road.

Gear

In this section, I'm going to cover the stuff that I carry plus additional items that most other riders might want to think about bringing along on the trip. One thing I won't cover in this section is camping equipment. I don't feel qualified to write about it because I personally don't camp on my trips. That said, if you are planning to camp, most of the gear I've listed in this section will still apply to you.

Cell Phone

You don't have to turn it on, but you should bring it with you. I use my smartphone for dozens of things while traveling. I use it for streaming music to my headset, directions, restaurant reviews, weather forecasts, texts, emails, hotel booking, alarm clock and the occasional phone call. Along with your cell phone, remember to bring your charger too.

Camera

You're going to see some amazing things, so be sure to bring a camera along with you on your trip. That may mean using the camera on your smartphone and that's fine. Smartphone cameras have come a long way and can take some excellent quality pictures and require no additional space. I use a combination of my smartphone and a quality point and shoot camera. If you have space, bring along your DSLR, fancy lenses and tripod but still be prepared to use your smartphone or point and shoot. The DSLR is not always going to be the most convenient. If you do a lot of walking at a destination you made decide to leave it on the bike. In those cases, the smaller camera is better than nothing.

Tablet or Laptop

For the last few years, I've been traveling with an iPad Mini. It doesn't take up much space, and it's great to checking out local restaurants once we get to the hotel for the evening. It's also great for researching things we are planning to see the next day. If you have Netflix or other streaming account you can also use it for watching tv.

The laptop can come in handy if you're shooting a lot of photos or videos. It will allow you to start editing or sharing your photos or footage while you're still on your trip. It will also allow you to back up all of your important files to another hard drive or the cloud so you don't have to worry about losing them.

Portable Charger

Portable chargers come in many sizes and price points. Some are powerful enough to jump start your motorcycle if you were to have a dead battery. I don't carry anything that heavy duty, but I do keep a portable charger on the bike. We have found it useful for charging the headsets at lunch, if we know we are going to be on the bike longer than the batteries typically last. They come in handy for giving your cell phone a quick bump in power or charging anything else when you don't have access to a wall outlet. Most don't take up more space than a typical smartphone, so they are definitely worth the space they occupy on the bike.

Stuff for your Bike

We are not going to be talking about things you can add to or put on your bike like we did at the beginning of this chapter. Instead, we are going to go over items your bike may need during the trip.

Bike Cleaner

You'd be surprised how many bugs can hit a face shield in a day. Sometimes I have to clean mine at lunch because it's already covered in bug guts and other road debris. Having a bottle of bike cleaner comes in handy to keep your face shield and windshield clean and clear.

At the end of each day, I also like to wipe down my bike before throwing the cover on it. Keeping bugs, tars and other foreign objects off the paint each day will help protect the finish and keep your bike looking better, longer. Keeping the paint free of dust and dirt will also protect it from scratching from things like your tank bag magnets and anything else that may rub across the paint.

Rags

Rags take up very little space and have various uses. For the most part, I use mine to clean off my helmet and my bike. You can also use them for blowing your nose or cleaning other things should you get stuck in the middle of nowhere and no place to "go."

I like microfiber towels because they are very soft and safe to use on almost all surfaces. You can buy bags of them from retailers such as Walmart for little cost. I use the newest ones on painted surfaces and then as they get soiled, they get used for things like cleaning brake dust off of wheels or wiping off road grime from metal surfaces before they are eventually thrown away. If you run out of clean rags on a trip, you can wash them. But, I find it easier and almost as inexpensive to buy a new small pack.

Tire Pressure Gauge

I can't overstress the importance of having your tires properly inflated. Pick up a small tire pressure gauge to keep on your bike or in your pocket. I'm aware that more and more bikes are coming equipped with TPMS, but you should still carry a gauge. Even if you end up not needing it, your riding buddy might.

Chain Lube

If your bike is chain drive, pack a small bottle of chain lube for the trip. Most manufacturers call for lubrication every 300-600 miles, so just plan on lubing it at the end of each day. If you get caught out in the rain, you may have to lube it a little sooner.

Kickstand Puck

A kickstand or side stand puck is used to help increase the surface area of your side stand to keep it from sinking into the ground. They are about the size of a hockey puck and usually made of a plastic or rubber material. They are commercially available or you can make your own. Kickstand pucks are especially useful when you have to park in the dirt, grass or on asphalt on a very hot day. Without a puck, I once had my bike sink over 2 inches into the asphalt. Fortunately, I got to it before it fell over.

It's also possible to make a plate for your center stand as well. I have one made out of a piece of diamond plate and it takes up very little space in my top case.

Additional Preparation

Before hopping on your bike to take off, there are still a few more things left to do before leaving for your trip.

Check the Weather Forecast

Keeping tabs on the most up-to-date weather information is of the utmost importance when traveling via motorcycle. As motorcyclists, we are far more exposed to weather conditions than just about any other form of travel. Knowing the weather forecast can help you when it comes to packing the right clothing for your trip. It can also help keep you safe by steering clear of any extreme weather conditions such as tornadoes, hurricanes, thunderstorms and snowstorms.

I've had to reroute trips in the past in order to avoid inclement weather. Kristen and I were once planning to ride through Aspen and Estes Park but when we reached Colorado Springs the weather in those areas was calling for heavy rain for three straight days. While we could have ridden through the rain, we would not have had visibility of the great views we dreamed of seeing. Therefore, I rerouted the trip to take in the Grand Canyon. Instead of spending three days getting peppered by rain, we had three days of great weather and amazing sights.

Check for Events

If you didn't do it while planning your trip initially, take a few minutes to check event calendars in any towns you may be planning to stay during your trip. You'll be surprised how quickly hotels can book up in midsize and smaller cities and towns when there is an event in the area. It doesn't even have to be a big event. One night I couldn't find a hotel room in Canton, Ohio, because there was a softball tournament in town. I ended up having to ride to Kent, Ohio to stay for the night. Most convention and visitor bureau websites have an up-to-date events' calendar on their websites. If you do see an event listed for the day you plan to be there and are unsure of how it will impact hotel availability, traffic, and restaurants, most have a contact page.

Check Hotel Availability

As I've mentioned a few times, I usually like to book my hotel rooms the same day. However, depending on where you are planning to stay, booking the same day isn't always possible. Sometimes you need to book months or even a year in advance in order to get the room you want. This is particularly true at many national parks and resorts. Places like Old Faithful Inn in Yellowstone National Park are usually booked a year in advance. Normally, a quick check online through a hotel booking site will tell you all you need to know about whether or not you should be concerned about finding a room in a particular town on a particular night. It only takes a few minutes to check, and it can save you a headache later.

Checklist

Start making a checklist a few days before you're planning to leave. Don't just include things you need to pack but also include things you need to do. You'll continue to add things to it as the date approaches. I make a checklist for all of my longer trips. I check things off the list as they are added to the bike or as the action is completed. With a good checklist, you won't forget anything. With no checklist, you'll forget all sorts of things.

Study Your Map

I know we discussed it in the previous chapter but use the last few days leading up to your trip to familiarize yourself with your route as much as possible. I like to think of my route as a good script. With a good script you can "ad-lib" along the way and still find your way back to your script to finish your story. A good route is the same way. You may have to deviate, or "ad-lib," from your route due to a road closing, accident or other unforeseen circumstance. Because you studied your map and have a route planned, if you are forced to deviate from it you'll be able to get back on it to finish your trip.

Plot Points

If you're planning to use GPS, take the days leading up to your trip to plot your points. If you type a town or destination into your GPS, in most cases it's going to give you the fastest route or the shortest route. I usually don't like either of those routes and tend to course my own. The trick is to select towns or places along the way that will force the GPS onto the roads and routes you want to travel. If I'm taking a multiple day trip, I plot points for each day. Even though I usually have my route memorized, I find plotting points on the GPS comes in handy. My GPS has features such as "search for gas stations on current route." By having the GPS route running, I can see things like gas stations on my current route instead of ones just in a certain vicinity (which in my cases are miles off of my route).

If you are going to plot points on your GPS, don't wait until the morning of your trip; get it done ahead of time. Also, throw a map or atlas in your tank bag. While GPS is great, it's always smart to carry a backup.

Conclusion

While it may seem like a lot of things to prepare, it's really not that bad, nor does it take a lot of time. Once you get a few trips under your belt, a lot of this will become second nature. In the forthcoming chapters, I'm going to discuss things you'll need to do on your trip and actions you'll take after your trip is complete. I've written this book as a guide to help you get started in motorcycle travel, but as with most things you'll learn the most by doing.

Chapter 7
During the Trip

It's finally time to head out on your long-awaited motorcycle adventure! In this chapter, I'm going to go over a few things you'll need to take into account before leaving and then discuss my tips and advice for making your trip as enjoyable as possible.

This chapter is going to jump around just a bit. It's going to begin with a section covering a few last items to tend to before you leave your house on day one and will then immediately jump to the morning of day two of your trip. I am not doing this to make things confusing. I believe the pre-ride checks before you leave your house are very important and far different than pre-ride checks and tips from day two through the rest of your trip.

Before You Leave

If you've already taken all the steps in the previous chapter to prepare yourself and your bike, there really isn't much left to do before taking off on your trip.

The Night Before

Go over your bike one last time. Check the highlights such as oil level and tire pressure. You don't want to be in for any surprises the next morning when you wake up. Also, do yourself a favor and top off your fuel tank. Unless you plan to meet some buddies at the gas station in the morning, it's best to leave your house on a full tank to get out of town as quickly as possible.

I prefer to have everything loaded on my bike the night before or at least have everything loaded in the bag liners and tank bag. About the only thing I don't have packed are things like my cell phone, the clothing I'll be wearing the next morning and my riding gear. Try to get a good night's sleep, which I will admit is sometimes difficult because you're so excited to start your trip.

Departure Day

Try to stick with your normal morning routine as much as possible. Drink your morning coffee and eat breakfast. Take a second to look over your route one final time and also be sure to check the weather report so you don't have any surprises.

Before Each Day's Ride

The first thing I do every morning is peek out the window of my hotel room to make sure my bike is still there. To date, it always has been. Next, I normally put on some pants and brush my teeth.

When I'm at home, I typically work out 5 to 6 days a week. When we are traveling, it's difficult to find the extra space to pack workout clothes. During my trip, I will try to get a body weight workout (dips, pushups, sit ups, etc.) completed in the room before eating breakfast. If you're a runner, many hotels have a treadmill or you can take a nice run outside as well. If you're planning to work out in the morning, just be sure to allot the time for both the workout and getting a shower.

Eat Breakfast

I like to stay at hotels that offer a hot breakfast (free or paid) or stay within walking distance of a restaurant or diner that serves breakfast. It doesn't always work out that way, but I recommend starting out each day with a hearty breakfast. If you're a coffee drinker, drink your coffee. While I'm not a coffee drinker myself, I do enjoy some caffeine in the morning. Also, be sure to drink some water at breakfast. It's important to stay hydrated. Make sure your belly is good and full before taking off in the morning; you're going to need the energy.

During or after breakfast, I like to look over the day's route once more and discuss it with my travel companions (which in most cases is just Kristen). I always check the weather. I don't want to be surprised by any weather changes that may have happened over night. If you have any battery-powered devices, this is your last chance to check to make sure they properly charged overnight.

Check Your Room

I know what I'm about to say is common sense, but once you think you have everything packed up go through your hotel room one more time to make sure you didn't forget anything. Don't forget to check the bathroom one last time as well. I make a point to double and triple check the room before I leave. The last thing I lost (forgot) was a GoPro battery and battery charger. I didn't remember it until after we got home.

Sunscreen

Even with a dark-tinted shield, applying some sunscreen on your face before you take off is a good idea. Don't forget to apply some to your neck as well. Since I wear a full-face helmet, gloves, jacket, long pants and boots, only my neck is fully exposed to the elements, but UV rays can still get through my face shield, especially when I have it cracked open a bit. If you don't ride in full gear, be sure to apply sunscreen to all exposed skin. While the wind may feel nice and cool, it'll also give you a false impression that you aren't burning your skin. I'm not a physician, but SPF 30 is what I use. Be sure to pick up some sort of "sport" formula since it'll hold up to sweating. You definitely want to avoid getting sunscreen in your eyes.

Look Over Your Bike

Before getting on your bike, there are still a few things you need to do. First, look at the ground under your bike to see if there is anything wet. If there is, check to see if it's oil, gas, coolant, etc. One morning we woke up in Lexington, Kentucky only to find oil under my buddy Thad's bike. We checked the oil level, and it was fine. We figured out that it had dripped from the breather tube and fortunately all was well. In any event, checking under the bike should be the first thing you do. It's also a good idea to check the oil glass (or dipstick). Give the bike a quick look over to ensure you don't see any leaks or other issues.

Ok, the bike is good and you're fueled up and ready to go. My last recommendation would be to get a light dynamic stretch in before taking off for the day. Dynamic stretching is stretching while moving including things like walking lunges with a twist, knee to chest, high kicks, arms circles, etc. The more limber you are, the longer you'll be able to sit on the bike without tightening up and getting sore.

During the Ride

Aside from paying attention to your surroundings and having fun, there are a few other things you'll need to do during the ride.

Clear Vision

Keep your face shield (or glasses/goggles) and your windshield clean. You'll be surprised how many bugs you'll run into during a few hundred miles. The more bugs or dirt you have covering your face or windshield, the worse your visibility gets. In most cases, I can get by with wiping my face shield down at lunch or in some cases not until after I'm finished riding for the day. However, there have been days where I've had to clean my face shield multiple times. The easiest time to clean it is when you stop for fuel or food. I don't remember a time when I've pulled over specifically to clean off my shield.

Fuel

Speaking of fuel, keep an eye on both your fuel gauge and your trip odometer. I've had too many fuel gauges betray me over the years, so I'm partial to the trip odometer (or odometer if you don't have a trip odometer). If you know your bike well, you know about how many miles it can go on a tank. I've gone through places in the West and Midwest where you can go over 100 miles without seeing a fuel station. Running out of fuel on my bike is not something I want to do, and I doubt you do either.

Stay Hydrated

If you wear a hydration system, you can obviously take care of your hydration on the go. I don't, so I always drink some water during fuel stops. I can't stress how important it is to stay hydrated during a long day of riding. I also make it a point to do some light stretching, particularly of my legs and shoulders when we stop for fuel anywhere else along the way. It's good to get some blood flowing through your muscles and make sure joints don't get too tight.

Keep Some Things Handy

Keep some cash, your sunglasses and a ball cap handy. I like to keep mine in the tank bag and have easy access to cash in case of tolls. You're also going to need cash (or a credit card) to get into parks and other destinations. Being able to access your wallet without having to dig into your pockets or get off of your bike will make your life (and those in line behind you) easier. Sunglasses are something I put on at almost every stop (maybe not fuel stops). I ride with a tinted shield, so if my helmet comes off the sunglasses go on. I keep mine easily accessible in my tank bag, so it only takes a second to find them. I also keep a ball cap (and in most cases Kristen's ball cap) in the tank bag as well. I like to throw on a hat for two reasons: 1) It hides my "helmet hair" 2) It helps keep the sun out of my eyes. If you're bald, you won't suffer from "helmet hair," but a ball cap may help protect your head from sunburn.

Lunchtime

I've read that stopping at "off times" for lunches can save some time, but I think it really depends on the day of the week, time of the year and your location. I prefer to stop when I'm hungry which is usually around noon. Taking some time off of the bike for a filling lunch will give you time to rid yourself of some riding gear, stretch out a little and relax. While I don't like to eat anything heavy for lunch, I do make sure I eat plenty. Riding will burn up more calories than you think, so it's important to fuel your body.

I like to take care of a few other things during lunch as well. I check the battery life on my cellphone and headset. I will occasionally take my wall charger into the restaurant if I need to charge something. In many cases, there is an outlet nearby. If I've been filming on my GoPro cameras, I normally switch out the batteries at lunch time. By lunchtime, I have a very good idea of whether we are on track to make our destination for the night, so I usually book my hotel before getting back on the bike. This is also an optimal time to check email, text messages, social media notifications and make a phone call. Checking the current weather report is also a good idea before continuing on your journey.

Weather

If you use a rain suit, always put it on before you think you'll need it. I've chanced it a few times, and I've almost always ended up wet. One time in Colorado, Kristen and I did manage to get the rain suits on before getting wet, but we had to pull over on a tiny road shoulder and it wasn't the safest. In most cases, if it's calling for rain or looks like rain, I'll find the first safe place to pull over and put on the suits. I've purchased new riding gear that's waterproof but haven't tested it yet.

Destinations/Points of Interest

A lot of what you'll do when you stop at different points of interest along the way will be dictated by the types of places you're stopping to check out. I'm going to offer a few suggestions. Be sure to take your camera (or phone if you're using its camera) with you and take lots of pictures. I use a small point-and-shoot style camera that I keep in a little bag which I clip onto the belt loop of my pants. You'll see a lot of cool things on your trip so be sure to capture some of them.

If you're going to be doing a lot of walking, you may want to change out of your riding boots and put on a pair of sneakers or more comfortable shoes. While my touring boots are pretty comfortable, they're also very heavy compared to a tennis shoe.

While it may be common sense, don't forget to take your wallet with you. I keep mine in one of the side pockets of my tank bag for comfort and convenience purposes. You'd be surprised how many times I've walked into a place only to have realized I left my wallet on the bike.

When it comes to valuables (headsets, GPS, helmets, etc), make sure to either take them with you or lock them in and/or on your bike. I lock my helmet on my bike but first pop off the headset and lock it in the trunk. If I have my GoPro mounted, it gets locked in the trunk as well. On hot days, I'll sometimes leave my jacket on the bike. To keep it out of view, I throw the half cover over my bike. I doubt many people are interested in stealing a motorcycle jacket covered in dirt and bugs, but the cover will keep people from seeing it anyway.

After the Ride

You may be finished riding for the day, but you still have a few things left to do before getting some rest.

When to Stop

I like to be at the hotel by 4:00 pm and no later than 5:00 pm. It doesn't always work out that way, but that's always my goal. I'm an early riser, so I'm normally on the road by 7:00 each morning. By getting off the bike by 4:00pm, I miss a lot of commuter traffic because most people haven't gotten off of work yet. Also, if you haven't booked your hotel ahead of time, getting into a town earlier will improve your chances of finding a room vacancy. If you're staying at a hotel with a pool, you'll have plenty of sunlight left to enjoy a swim before dinner. Additionally, I don't care to ride at night, so that's yet another reason I'm off the bike earlier in the day.

Starting early and ending early won't be for everyone, but it's what I have found works best for me most of the time. If you're going to ride during different times, just take into account how that may affect other aspects of your trip. If you're planning to ride until 9:00 each night, you may need to think about booking a hotel earlier in the day. Conversely, stopping too early in the afternoon may also cause problems, as most hotels won't allow you to check-in until 3:00 pm at the earliest.

Picking a Parking Space

Once you've checked into your room for the night, you'll need to pick out a parking space. When I stay at motels with outward facing rooms, I try to get on the first floor so I can park my bike in the space right in front of my door. If I am unable to get the first floor room, I will still park my bike as near to the room as possible.

Hotels can be a tad trickier since the rooms face inward. In most cases I park my bike so I have a view of it from my hotel window. However, if that puts the bike on the backside of the building or in an area I don't feel is safe, I will park it somewhere else. I have seen many riders park their bikes near the front door under an overhang. I've only done that once and it was because I had been riding in a downpour for the last hour. It was still raining when I rolled into the lot, and the rest of the parking lot was beginning to flood. I don't like parking my bike under the overhang for two reasons: 1) It's more likely someone will bump into it with their car when they pull up to check-in 2) Too many curious people walking by that may decide to sit on it (though I keep a cover on mine).

Unloading

Once parked, I like to immediately get everything unloaded from the bike. The helmets, tank bag and GPS are the first items we take to the room. Kristen and I are able to grab both bag liners out of the saddlebags on the first trip as well. My trunk/top case normally has a few things I may need like the atlas or layer I had peeled off earlier in the day.

Clean the Bike

Sometimes I may hit the pool first or lounge around in the room for a bit. But in most cases, once all of our gear is in the hotel room, I head back outside to start cleaning up the bike. I always travel with a bottle of spray polish/cleaner and some microfiber towels. The windshield and front of the bike including the headlight(s) and front fender take the brunt of the damage when it comes to bugs and filth. Once I've finished cleaning up the front of my bike, I wipe down any other areas that may have gotten some dust or bugs on them. The whole process normally take less than five minutes and keeps my bike looking nice and clean during the duration of my trip.

Maintenance & Checks

If your bike is chain drive, now is the best time to keep and/or lube your chain. Chain lube will stick to a chain best while it's still warm. Allowing the lube to sit overnight, it'll be less likely to fling off and onto your rear wheel.

Also, use this time to check both tires for wear as well as nails or other metal that may have penetrated them. It never hurts to check the oil and other fluids either.

Cover It Up

Once I'm finished cleaning and going over the bike, it's almost time to throw the cover on it. Before installing the cover, make sure you've got everything you need off of the bike including the spray cleaner and a towel (you're going to need it again in a few minutes).

Back in the Room

Next, I get the face shields and helmets wiped down and cleaned. Kristen's normally isn't too bad, but mine is always covered in bugs. The longer they're on the helmet, the harder they are to get off so clean it up as soon as you can. I like to get the headsets on the charger next. Normally, they only take a couple of hours to charge.

I enjoy kicking off my riding boots and getting out of my riding gear. I like to get into a change of comfortable clothes as soon as possible. A dip in the pool or a shower can do wonders.

While lounging around in the room, I use the Yelp app on my tablet or smartphone to check out nearby restaurants and bars in an attempt to find a good place to eat that evening. Another good source for restaurant recommendations is the person at the front desk of the hotel. They are usually friendly and in most cases will be very helpful at making recommendations. Look at your room key or check with the front desk about discounts as well. Your hotel may have a deal with some local restaurants where you just have to show your key, and you'll save a certain percentage off your bill. If you're particularly tired after a long day of riding, there's nothing wrong with having some takeout delivered to your room.

Dinner

National restaurant chains are consistent in the quality of food and atmosphere they provide. With few exceptions, you know what to expect when you walk inside one. National chains are a safe bet as a dining option when you're traveling, but they aren't the most fun. I really like Texas Roadhouse, but there's one 10 minutes from my house so it's not the most exciting option when I'm 500 miles from home in a place I may never visit again.

When Kristen and I are traveling, we like to try out the local favorites. Reviews on Yelp, Facebook, Google and other sites can help you make a more informed decision about where to dine. We've even planned ahead to eat at a certain place we found while planning the trip. We've had a few misses when it comes to picking out restaurants, but the overwhelming majority of our picks work out well. My mouth still waters thinking about the Snake River Farms Beef Zabuton I had one night at the Million Dollar Cowboy Steakhouse in Jackson Hole, WY.

Get Some Rest

I try to fully enjoy the time I spend in each place we stay. It doesn't matter if it's a big city or small map dot, you're (almost) always going to be able to find a place to have fun. That said, make sure you get plenty of rest. Riding can and will take a lot out of you. I try to get between 7-9 hours of rest per night. I've ridden on much less sleep than that and while adrenaline will keep you going for a while, it'll eventually run out and make for a less than spectacular day of riding.

Conclusion

The takeaway from this chapter is a very simple one; take care of yourself and take care of your bike. The good news is that most modern motorcycles are reliable, so I wouldn't worry too much about the bike. If you just do the simple things I suggested in this chapter, your bike should be fine.

Keep yourself hydrated, nourished and limber. Drink more water than you think you need, don't skimp on eating and take a minute or two to stretch out when you stop. If I had any final advice, it's to take it easy on the alcohol. Riding your motorcycle for 400 miles is fun. Riding your motorcycle for 400 miles with a hangover isn't much fun.

Chapter 8
After the Trip

Sadly, all motorcycle trips must come to an end. In this chapter, I'm going to go over some steps to take once you return home from your trip. While some of these steps are meant for those coming back from week long or longer trips, most of the information will also apply to shorter trips as well.

The First 24 Hours

The final day of my trip is usually a high mileage day, so I'm pretty tired when I arrive back at my house. As much as I would just like to go inside and fall on the couch, there are a few things I always do and recommend you do as well before passing out.

Unpack the Bike

Before I even change out of my riding gear, I take the bag liners in the house, remove the tank bag and clear the top case of anything that I don't normally keep in it. I do this before changing out of my gear because to get out of all of my gear normally requires me to sit down. I know if I sit down I'm not going to want to get back up.

Riding Gear

Clean your helmet before putting it away. You've done this every day of your trip, so it should be ingrained into your routine at this point. Since it may be a few days before you ride again, you don't want all the bugs and dirt hardening on your helmet. It'll only make it more difficult to remove if you wait a few days.

Hang up your riding gear. Even if you plan on washing it, hang it up first. I'll explain my reasoning for this later in the chapter.

Rest

Get a nice, hot shower, change into some comfortable clothes and rest. Motorcycle travel is a lot of fun, but it's also tiring. Take at least the rest of the day to do nothing more than lounge around. Catch up on your favorite TV shows, read some magazines that came in the mail since you left or just take a nap. I normally just take off the rest of the evening, but on more strenuous rides I may take close to 24 hours before I do much.

The Next 24 Hours

Whether you got a full 24 hours of rest or just a nice evening of doing nothing followed by a good night's sleep, hopefully you feel refreshed and rested. The bad news is some of the tasks we have left to complete are not much fun. The good news is most of the tasks won't take long.

Check Your Gear

Remember how I told you not to wash your gear yet and to just hang it up? It's time to explain why. Depending on the type of riding gear you wear, you may not have to wash it or it may not even be machine washable. With it hanging on a hanger, take a few minutes to give it a really good inspection. See if you can find any seams that are starting to come apart, areas that are becoming worn, or just general deterioration. A few thousand miles of riding can really cause some wear and tear on your gear. Be sure to flip your jacket and pants inside out to inspect any linings your suit may have. If everything looks good, follow the manufacturer's care instructions to clean your jacket and pants.

Riding gloves tend to wear out faster than the rest of riding gear. Again, look for any seams that may be splitting, worn padding or check for fraying if they have mesh. Most gloves can't be washed, so put them away if they are in good shape.

Boots should only take you a minute or two to inspect. Check the soles to see if they're worn. If they look good, just clean them up a bit and put them back in the closet until it's time to ride again.

Even though you gave your helmet a good polishing after you got home, go pull it back out of the cabinet or closet where you keep it because we need to inspect it as well. Check the outer shell to make sure there aren't any cracks or deep scratches. Once you've inspected the outside, check the liner. If it's looking dirty or starting to stink, check the manufacturer's recommendations for cleaning the liner. I've replaced the cheek pads in mine which is usually a pretty nominal cost. The last thing to check is the visor. Give it a good look from the outside and put the helmet on and look through it. Rocks or pieces of road debris can scratch or nick a visor deep enough to partially obstruct your view. When this happens, I replace the visor.

Unpack

Ugh, unpacking sucks. The good news for you is you only packed a small bag liner so it won't take long. In addition to your clothing, it's time to triage all the souvenirs and trinkets you bought on your trip. Don't forget to unload your tank bag and put all of that stuff away as well. Once you've got everything unloaded and thrown it in the wash, put your bag liners and tank bag back wherever they belong so you'll be able to find them for your next trip.

Data Backup

If you took pictures or videos (and I hope you did), BACK THEM UP! If you backed up your data to the cloud, a computer, or an external hard drive along the way, great. If not, you need to make sure you back up all of your data. You made some awesome memories on this trip, so you don't want to lose all of the wonderful images you took just because a memory card fails or you happen to lose your phone.

The Next 48 Hours & Beyond

It has probably set in by now that you've successfully completed your motorcycle trip and made it home safely. If you're anything like me you're already thinking about your next one. However, before you start planning your next trip you need to go back out to the garage to see your bike first.

Your Bike

I have some friends that will wash their bike as soon as they get home...I don't. It's normally a day or two after I return from a long trip before I will get the bike back out of the garage. Even if you wiped your bike down every day of your trip, it's still going to be dirty enough to deserve a good bath. Once you're done washing and drying your bike, be sure to check all the normal things such as tire wear, chain adjustment, leaks, etc.

Depending how many miles you rode, it may be time to do some routine maintenance on your bike such as an oil change, spark plug replacement or valve clearance inspection. You'll need to consult your owner's manual to see when these services are due. If you don't do your own maintenance, get it scheduled with your dealer or mechanic as soon as possible. During spring and summer, it could take a while to get your bike in for service so don't wait until the last minute. If you do your own maintenance, pick up the fluids and parts you're going to need and schedule some time on your calendar to get the work done.

Notes & Planning

I take a small notebook along on my trip to make notes about things I saw or experienced throughout each day. If you didn't take any notes, that's ok. Now is your chance to start making notes. You can make notes about anything and everything. Did you pass by a place that you didn't get to stop and hang out? Write it down. Did you realize you need a bigger tank bag? Write it down. Were back to back 500-mile riding days too much? Write it down.

You need to write down anything and everything you learned on your trip; things you liked about it, things you want to change next time you take a trip, things you want to do to your bike and anything else or any other idea you want to write down. Writing all of this stuff down within a day or two after your trip is important because everything is still fresh in your mind. Using these notes to help plan your next trip will make your next trip even better.

Chapter 9
Tips and Tricks

    Chapter 9 is going to comprise all the tips and tricks to motorcycle travel that I couldn't fit into the first eight chapters of the book. I will touch on some things that I mentioned earlier in the book because I either a) feel like they are important enough that they need to be mentioned twice or b) further detail is needed. I will also go over various tips, tricks and hacks that haven't yet been mentioned.

Stuff to Pack

    Some of these items were mentioned in Chapter 6 along with many other essential things you'll need to pack. The following items other things you may want to consider packing and why you may want them.

Pain Reliever

    I prefer ibuprofen while Kristen prefers naproxen. I'm not a physician so please don't take any medical advice from me. That said, I find it beneficial to bring along a small amount of pain reliever to help with aches, pains, and headaches that may be experienced along the way. You may also find it'll come in very handy if you happen to drink too much the night before. While I know you can buy it along the way, a small pack at a convenience store can run a few bucks as opposed to a few cents if you're bringing them from home. Besides, they don't take up much room on the bike.

Other Medications

    If you're on prescription medications or other over-the-counter medications, remember to pack them. Check with your pharmacist and/or doctor ahead of time in the event you'll need a medication refilled before returning from your trip.

Toll Pass

If you're going to be traveling on any toll roads, I would highly suggest bringing your toll pass along. Trying to pay with cash at a toll booth while riding a motorcycle can be a real pain and take much longer than it does in a car. I've found that placing my toll pass in the map section of my tank bag allows the toll booth sensors to pick it up just fine.

Notebook

I know I said you can take notes on your mobile device but I still prefer an old school notebook. They're dirt cheap and take up almost no space. There's also no battery to go dead on them and they don't break. I suppose in an emergency they could also come in handy "if nature calls," but that's not why I'm suggesting you bring one along. I like to keep track of the mileage I travel each day and the total mileage of the trip. I also write down the town we stop in each night. Sometimes I'll write down where we ate or the hotel we stayed at if there was something that stood out about it. It's your notebook, so you can write whatever you like in it. I think it's a good idea to have something to track your thoughts throughout the trip. The more stuff you write down, the less stuff you'll forget when you get home.

Charging Cables

Don't forget your charging cables. I have little labels on all of mine so I can tell them apart. It also makes it easier to tell if I've packed the right ones. Bring at least one cable for each device. A battery-powered device isn't much good if you are unable to charge it. While most cables can be found at Walmart or even convenience stores now, it's just easier and cheaper to bring them with you.

Portable Charger

A portable charger is basically a battery pack. I have one that isn't much bigger than a smartphone but will charge my iPhone about 8 times or my MacBook 1.5x times before the charger itself needs to be recharged. It'll also allow you to plug in 2 USB devices at a time for charging. Manufacturers make larger ones and smaller ones at many different price points. I bought mine for around $30 in the spring of 2016.

I've used my portable charger to give my phone or Bluetooth headset a boost when I stop for lunch if a wall outlet isn't available or conveniently located. I've also left GoPro batteries in my top case to charge when we are checking out a park, museum or point of interest on our trip. Whether you buy one or not, I would suggest checking them out.

USB Wall Charger

I bought an inexpensive 4-port USB wall charger to use when traveling. Unfortunately, most hotels rooms don't have many wall outlets available. The USB wall charger will allow me to plug in up to 4 USB devices to charge at once while only taking up one wall outlet. It doesn't take up much room, as it's about the size of a pack of playing cards. Since we normally have 2 headsets and 2 cell phones to charge, the small charger works perfect.

iPad/Tablet

I bring along my iPad Mini which only has wifi connectivity. Kristen and I use it mostly for scoping out local restaurants once we get checked into the hotel. With a larger screen than my phone, it also makes it more convenient if I need to do some research for the next day's ride like looking at weather or road maps. You can also load the Netflix or Amazon Video apps, or if you're a MotoGP fan the VideoPass app so you don't miss any racing action. I also like using the iPad for FaceTime when calling home to talk to my son.

Credit Card

Bring at least one credit card. You can bring your debit card along, but you also need a credit card. There is a reason I'm repeating the word credit card, because you need to bring one. The main reason you need to bring a credit card is for booking hotel rooms. Hotels routinely put a $50-$200 per day "hold" on your credit card for incidentals. You can think of it as a security deposit. While the charge is normally gone after 24-48 hours, if you're using a debit card it can affect the amount of money accessible in your checking account. You can still use your debit card to pay for the room, but I would suggest using a credit card to be placed on hold for incidentals so you don't tie up any of the funds you may need for the rest of your trip.

If you're traveling with someone else who is handling all of the bookings, I still recommend bringing along a credit card. Even if you don't plan to charge a single purchase, it's still good to have one in case of an emergency.

Cash

There are still places that don't accept credit cards. On trips 3 days or less, I take about $60 cash. On longer trips, I bring along about $100. You may need cash for things like tolls (if you don't have a toll pass or the *correct* toll pass), entry fees to parks or museums, gas stations, and restaurants. I don't recommend carrying a lot of cash, but I've found around $100 to be a good starting point for longer trips.

Camera

A camera is a great way to share your trip with others when you get home or capture memories that you'll want to look back through yourself. Most people these days use their smartphone to take pictures which makes total sense because you're always carrying it with you, and most of them these days take excellent pictures. I still like to carry a nice point and shoot because it'll allow me to make more adjustments than most smartphones and has a better lens. Some riders like to travel with DSLR cameras with multiple lenses. If you have the space on your bike, you can capture some awesome images with that sort of equipment. If you are planning to take a camera other than your smartphone, be sure to pack some extra batteries. Most camera batteries are not readily available without visiting a specialty store.

Spare Key

Many riders and publications recommend traveling with a spare key (or fob) for your bike which is a really good idea. However, I'm going to have to put this tip under the "do as I say, not as I do" category, because I don't travel with a spare key. I suppose I could and should, but I subscribe to the "don't lose your key" philosophy instead. With a quick internet search, you can find some key hiding gizmos or if you're traveling with a buddy give him your spare to hold.

Bungee Net

I always have a bungee net under my seat or in my top case. Bungee nets are the ultimate motorcycle accessory. A bungee net will cost you under $10, takes up little space and lasts a long time. I've used my bungee to strap my helmet on the backseat (while riding around Key West), transport a case of beer and strap a skid plate to my seat. Because of the way they're made and how much they stretch, you can use a bungee to tie just about anything to your bike. A bungee net is something that's not only great to have while traveling but something you'll find plenty of use for while riding around town.

Passport

If you're going to be near the northern or southern border, take your passport with you. Even if you don't plan to cross the border, it's nice to have the option. When I recently renewed my passport, I decided to get the passport card along with it. The great thing about the passport card is that it will allow you in and out of Canada and Mexico without having to bring along your full-size passport. Since it slides into my wallet, it also requires no extra space. The passport card may be something to consider the next time your passport is up for renewal.

Flask

If you ride much in the south, you know there are many dry counties and jurisdictions. If you're unfamiliar with the term "dry county," it refers to a county, town or area where the sale of alcohol is prohibited. That means you can't buy beer, wine or liquor in that area. While dry counties can be found all across the country, the south has the highest concentration. If you enjoy a drink after your ride, I recommend carrying a flask filled with your favorite spirit.

In addition to totally dry areas, you'll also run into all sorts of other strange alcohol laws. For instance, in Maryland you won't find beer or wine in a grocery or convenience store. You can only buy alcohol from "liquor stores." In West Virginia, you can't buy alcohol on Sunday before 1:00pm and there are no retail liquor sales on Sundays. I recommend doing a quick Google search to find out the rules of the local area you'll be staying so you won't be surprised.

Securing Your Bike

If my car got stolen, I don't think I'd really care. It would be a bit of a pain to deal with the insurance company, but I don't have any sort of emotional attachment to my car and there are plenty of cars available to rent while I get mine replaced. If my motorcycle got stolen, I'd be pissed. If my motorcycle got stolen while I was on a trip, I'd be devastated. In this section, I'm going to give you some tips to keep your motorcycle safe while traveling.

Restaurants

Whenever you stop to eat, keep your bike in view at all times. When we go into a restaurant, I will ask the hostess to seat me where I can see my bike. I've never had an issue with them granting my request. If I eat at a restaurant in a downtown area where parking in front of the restaurant isn't possible or perhaps it's not possible to see my bike from inside, I park in a garage or a monitored lot. The garages with attendants are the safest, but even those without an attendant can keep your bike safer than parking it on the street.

Cover

I highly suggest you use a bike cover. A lightweight piece of nylon with an elastic band around the bottle of it is one of the best ways to protect your bike. It'll protect your bike from UV rays and rain, but it also acts like a very strong force field to keep people off and away from your machine. If you've never used a cover, you probably think I'm kidding but I can promise you I'm not. My only recommendation would be to not use a cover with the brand or make of the bike written on it unless it says Gold Wing; no one ever steals those things.

Securing Your Helmet

Most motorcycles are outfitted with a helmet lock, so be sure to use it when you're going to be away from your bike. The only exception would be at night when you should take your helmet into your hotel room. Strangely, my Yamaha FJR1300 didn't have a helmet lock (I suppose because each saddlebag could fit a full face helmet but that still makes no sense since it's a touring bike), so I had to come up with another solution. I ended up purchasing a *Helmetlok* rubberized, carabiner-type lock that allowed a 4-digit combination. In order to lock two helmets on the bike, I also purchased their optional coiled security cable. If your bike doesn't have a built in helmet lock, *Helmetlok* is worth a look. A locking top case or saddlebag will be the most secure way to protect your helmet from theft.

Securing Everything Else

Don't forget to remove the Bluetooth headset piece from your helmet and either take it with you or lock it in a saddlebag or top case. They are expensive and very easy to steal. Additionally, if you're like me and have a GoPro or other action camera mounted on your helmet, be sure to secure it as well.

Lock up or take anything else expensive with you. Do not leave items such as GPS, smartphones, or cameras unsecured on the bike. There is one expensive item I will occasionally leave behind on my bike, and that's my riding jacket. I only do this on hot days when I'm going to be walking around for a while. I feel comfortable leaving my jacket behind because I put my cover on the bike.

Hotel Parking

I know I went over this in Chapter 7 but I want to touch on it again. If at all possible, park your bike in front of your hotel/motel room door or as close by as possible. One thing I didn't touch on in Chapter 7 is valet parking a motorcycle. In some larger cities, they only have garage parking and some won't allow motorcycles. In those cases, the hotel will ask you to "valet" park your bike. I've yet to see a valet park a motorcycle nor would I let one. Valet parking of a motorcycle means (you) parking it in one of the valet spots. I've yet to be charged to park there, but I will tip the valet for keeping an eye on my bike all night. As always, I put the cover on it.

Apps

The last figure I saw indicated that there are 1,000 apps added to the Apple App Store every day. I'm sure the Google Play store is similar. While it would be impossible to include every travel or motorcycle-specific app in this book, I feel it important to share a few apps that I find useful.

Social Media Apps

I'm talking about Facebook, Twitter, Instagram, Snapchat, Pinterest and any other social media platform that may now exist since the publishing of this book. Social media apps are a great way to share pictures of your trip with friends and family. You'll be surprised how many people will comment with a suggestion of a place to stay, restaurant to try and other random thing to check out. I am unable to make it to most of the places people suggest, so I write them down in my notebook as ideas for future trips.

Insurance App

Hopefully you never have to use it, but downloading your insurance company's app to your phone is a smart idea. My insurance company has had an app for years, and they are continuously improving it. Most large insurance companies now have an app. The apps are always changing, but at minimum they'll allow you to access your policy information and in some cases you can even file a claim in the case of an accident or theft. Do a quick search in the app store or contact your insurance company to find what if your company offers one.

Review Apps

I use both the Yelp app and Yelp.com while planning my trip to read reviews on hotels, restaurants and destinations. TripAdvisor is another great source and there are many more out there. You'll have to weed through some garbage reviews, but for the most part they can provide you with some pretty good insight when trying to decide on a place to stay, eat or visit. While I can only speak to the Yelp app since it's the one I use, I really like the proximity feature that'll allow me to filter restaurants within a certain radius. Apps and websites can come in handy when you're visiting a place you've never been.

Web Browser

All smart phones come with a native web browser. Safari, Chrome, and Firefox are by far the most popular but there are other options available. I am including the web browser app because it's such a workhorse and often overlooked. While there is an app for almost everything these days, the web browser app is probably the most powerful of them all.

Hotel Booking Apps

There are plenty of hotel and travel booking apps to choose from including Priceline, Expedia, HotelTonight and many more. My personal favorite is Hotels.com. I've been using it for years and absolutely love it. While I'm a member of a few different hotel rewards programs, the rewards program with

Hotels.com is the easiest for me to use. After 10 stays, you get a night free; it's that simple. They have a great selection of hotel choices, a user-friendly app, and competitive pricing.

GPS Apps

If you don't have a GPS on your bike, you may rely on the GPS your smartphone provides. Apple Maps caught a lot of flak when it first came out, but it has improved. Other common GPS apps include Google Maps, MapQuest and one of the most talked about, Waze. Waze is owned by Google but remains a separate app from Google Maps. Waze's claim to fame is the user-generated traffic information that'll keep you informed of the location and severity of traffic. There are some other GPS apps on the market as well. It's worth the time to check them out.

Music Apps

If you have a headset in your helmet, you probably bought it at least in part so you could listen to music. When I got my first iPhone in 2008, the only app available to play music was the iTunes app. There are now dozens of different music apps available for your smartphone. Google Play Music and Apple Music are free built-in apps that come on Android and iPhone, respectively. Other apps include YouTube music, Shazam, Spotify, Amazon Music, Vevo, Soundcloud, Pandora and iHeartRadio. While not a music app per se, Podcast apps and audio book apps are also something to consider having on your phone to listen to while riding. Kristen will normally download a book to listen to on multi-day trips.

If you use a music streaming service, there are two things to be aware of: 1) your data plan 2) cell service interruptions throughout the country. I have unlimited data, so I'm not concerned about how much data I use when I'm streaming music. However, there are areas where I receive poor or no cell reception, so it's beneficial to have music downloaded directly to your phone.

Video Streaming

While I recommend checking out the local area you're staying, on some nights of longer trips you're either tired or you may end up in a place with little to no nightlife options. In those cases, apps such as Hulu, YouTube, Amazon Prime video or Netflix on your tablet or mobile device are handy. Unfortunately, not every hotel has the greatest choice of television channels. If you have your mobile device or tablet loaded with your favorite streaming app, it won't matter. You'll still be able to watch a great movie or your favorite TV series.

E-Reader Apps

I prefer a paper or hard backed book, but there isn't much space to pack one on a motorcycle trip. By using apps like Kindle, iBooks, Nook, or Scribd, you can bring dozens of books along on your trip and they all fit on your smartphone or tablet.

Video Call Apps

Video calls are a great way to stay in contact with loved ones back home. Since I'm an iPhone user, I've always used the built-in FaceTime app for video calls. While there are many video call apps and services, Skype is one of the most popular. If you're planning to use a video call app on your trip, make sure the people you want to call have a compatible device before leaving on your trip.

Lyft/Uber

When Kristen and I travel on the bike, I try to get a hotel that's within walking distance of a few restaurants or the area we plan to hang out for the evening. Unfortunately, it doesn't always work out that way so it leaves us with two options: 1) Ride the bike 2) Get a ride.

I'm a big fan of using Lyft or Uber when I'm out of town and want to get someplace that's too far to walk. Occasionally, we'll have to take the bike when we're in an area where these services aren't available, but I always try to leave the bike parked for the night once I get to the hotel. If I ride that bike, that means no drinking. If you haven't tried Uber or Lyft, I would recommend giving them a shot.

Souvenirs

Almost every place you stop will have all sorts of souvenirs available to buy. Most everyone has some sort of item or items he or she likes to collect. I've started collecting metal signs to hang in my garage. Kristen has built an impressive Starbuck's *You Are Here* mug collection. While I wouldn't say we "collect" them, t-shirts are another item we frequently buy while traveling.

Kristen's Mug Collection

Buying souvenirs while traveling on a motorcycle requires a bit of planning. I remember being on top of Pikes Peak looking at a Bigfoot crossing sign and wondering if it would fit in my top case. Since they had a strict no-return policy, I asked the clerk if I could take the sign out to my bike to see if it would fit in my top case. The store manager obliged, the sign fit and I bought it. Some stores will offer shipping on products, so it may be in your best interest to have the store ship your item to your home.

FedEx and UPS stores are another option should you buy more stuff than you can pack on your bike. During one ten-day trip, Kristen bought 9 Starbucks mugs. Fortunately, we crossed paths with my aunt and uncle who were also on a motorcycle trip. My uncle had space on his bike to take 4 or 5 mugs, so we were able to unload what she'd collected to that point allowing us to pick up the other 4 or 5 during the rest of the trip. Had my uncle not helped us out, we had planned to swing by a FedEx store that morning and ship them home. If you're riding with a buddy or group of riders, their additional storage may be an option. On one trip, my buddy Thad had run out of space to pack things on his bike so more and more of his stuff ended up in my tank bag.

Local Laws

When traveling to different states, I recommend doing some additional research or at the very least paying very close attention to posted laws. For instance, in some areas motorcycles are allowed to ride in the HOV lanes while in other places they are not. You're not allowed to pump your own gas in New Jersey. Riding through New York City? It's illegal to make a right on red unless the sign indicates otherwise. These are just a few examples of things you may experience while traveling to different areas throughout the US.

Helmet laws are also something you'll need to pay particular attention. While I ride with my helmet on 99.9% of the time, occasionally I'll leave mine in the hotel room if I'm riding around in a downtown area. Helmet laws vary state to state, ranging from mandatory requirement to no law to certain age restrictions and everything in between. The Insurance Institute for Highway Safety website is an excellent source for up-to-date information on helmet laws.

Most blue laws these days have to do with restrictions on alcohol sales. There are some other blue laws still on the books, but I don't think being prohibited from buying a vehicle on a Sunday in the state of Colorado is going to affect you on your next motorcycle trip. Alcohol sales vary from state to state and even county to county. Many counties in the south are still dry, meaning they don't sell alcohol at all. If you're not a drinker, that won't affect you.

Other Tips, Tricks & Hacks

Google or search on YouTube for "travel hacks" and you'll find thousands of listings. The tips, tricks and hacks that follow are things I've discovered along the way. While this is a motorcycle travel book, you may find some of these ideas will work for other forms of travel as well.

Roll Your Clothes

I roll all of my clothing when packing (except my socks). I roll my t-shirts, underwear and pants. There are two main reason to roll your clothes 1) They'll take up less space 2) They'll be less prone to wrinkle. To be honest, the less wrinkles are just a bonus. I'm much more interested in my clothing taking up as little space as possible, since space is highly coveted on a motorcycle. I'm not going to go into detail on how to roll your clothing, but a quick Google search should provide you with plenty of how-to videos.

Don't Waste Space

If you're packing a pair of sneakers, make them earn their space in your saddlebag. Instead of allowing my sneakers to waste any space, I'll stick my socks or any other small items into my shoes to help optimize my packing space.

Laundry

When you ride hundreds of miles each day exposed to the elements, your clothes aren't going to stay clean or fresh for long. Check the closet or bathroom of your hotel room for a plastic laundry bag. I put my dirty clothes in the bag to keep them from stinking up my clean clothes when everything goes back in the saddlebags. Moving the dirty clothes into the bag each day helps make laundry day easy since everything is gathered and ready to go.

When it comes to laundry, I'll buy detergent from the front desk or from the laundromat. If you don't want to have to buy it on the road, put some in a Ziploc bag (double bag for safety) and keep it with your toiletries. It'll take up almost no space and you wouldn't have to buy detergent on your trip.

Hand Towels & Washcloths

Earlier in the book, I discussed how I bring microfiber towels along to clean my helmet, bike and other gear. If for some reason you forget to bring towels, run out of clean towels or just decide to not bring any, you can use the hotel towels and washcloths to clean off your helmet and riding gear. DO NOT use the hotel towels on your bike. Using the hotel towels and washcloths on your bike is a bad idea for two reasons: 1) Many hotel towels aren't very soft and could scratch the finish on your bike 2) Leaving towels covered in grease and oil will only give motorcyclists a bad name. However, using them to wipe off your helmet or riding jacket will help keep your gear clean and won't do any damage to the hotel's property.

On a side note, occasionally you'll get lucky and stay at a "motorcycle friendly" hotel. These hotels will provide you with access to a water hose, bucket, and plenty of towels to wash and dry your bike. Hotels like this aren't easy to find, but they do exist.

USB Charging

If you only brought your USB cable but forgot to bring the wall outlet adapter to charge your device, you may still be in luck. If you have a flat screen in your hotel room, turn it around. Most modern televisions have a USB input. Plug your device into the USB input to charge.

ATM Fees

Miscalculations happen. You thought $80 cash would last the entire trip, but with two days to go you're down to $5. Fortunately, ATMs are pretty easy to find. Unfortunately, if you can't find one for your specific bank, foreign ATMs can charge a pretty hefty fee, plus your bank may hit you with a fee as well.

If you'd like to avoid paying fees to get cash, find a Walmart, grocery store or pharmacy. Almost any of them will allow you to get cash back on a purchase. Many retailers have a limit per transaction and policies will vary. While you'll have to make a purchase (pack of gum or maybe something you needed or were going to buy anyway), you won't be charged a fee by the store and in most cases your bank won't charge you any fees either.

Reward Points

Travel is an excellent opportunity to maximize your rewards point earnings on your credit card. I use my American Express Premier Rewards card for most of the purchases on our trips. I earn 2x points for purchases at restaurants and gas stations. It's also possible to earn 2x points at certain hotels. For all other purchases, I get one point per dollar spent. See what your credit or charge card earns you. If you find it's not offering much in return, you may want to consider switching to a card that's better in line with the types of purchases you make.

Reward points aren't just limited to credit cards. Most hotel chains, restaurants and gas stations now have reward programs. Participating in these programs can save you a decent amount of money over time and earn you some pretty cool perks. If you're new to travel, take an hour one evening to check out some different travel-specific rewards programs. If you're an experienced traveler (even if not on a motorcycle) you may already be a member of many of these types of programs; just don't forget to take advantage of them.

Conclusion

I hope you find these tips, tricks and hacks as useful on your trips as I have on my own. I learn something new every time I travel. Feel free to use any or all of the ideas I've shared with you and add in your own ideas as well. If you come up with something really cool, shoot me an email (Contact information is in the Intro). I'd love to hear about it.

Epilogue
Write Your Own Chapter

I want to sincerely thank you for purchasing (or at least reading) this book. I hope you've enjoyed the previous nine chapters and found them informative. As my writing comes to an end it's now time for you to write your own chapter. I want you to take the information I've shared and use it to plan and take your own dream motorcycle trip. I want you to have as much fun touring on your motorcycle as I do. I want you to know that you'll only have one regret after your first motorcycle trip...that you didn't do it sooner.

I look forward to seeing you on the road. Ride safe and have fun!

All the Best,

Mario

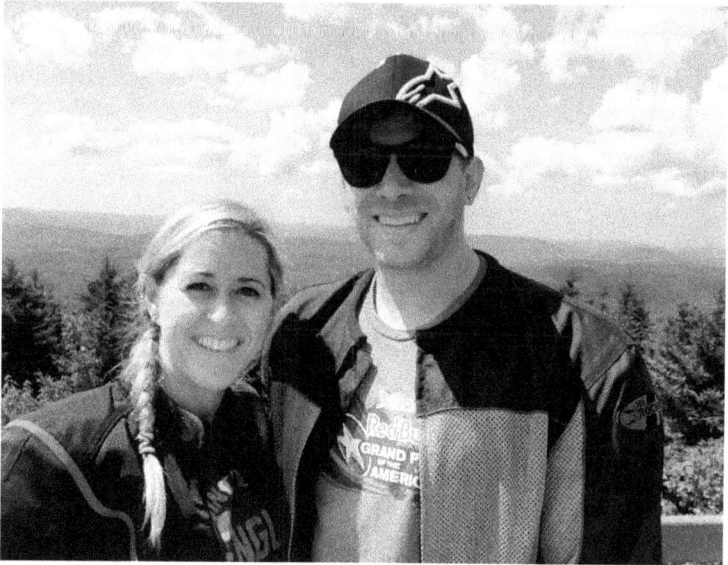

References

Illminen, G. (2013, April 8). Motorcycle Helmet Standards Explained: DOT, ECE 22.05 & Snell. Retrieved March 2, 2017, from https://ultimatemotorcycling.com/2013/04/08/motorcycle-helmet-standards-explained-dot-ece-22-05-snell/

Smith, J. (2013, May 16) CE or Not CE? The Hard Truth About Armor. Retrieved March 2, 2017, from http://www.motorcyclistonline.com/how-to/hard-truth-about-armor-ce-or-not-ce

Tibu, F. (2014, June 23). BMW USA Announces Compensations for Customers Affected by the 2014 R1200RT Recall. Retrieved March 2, 2017, from https://www.autoevolution.com/news/bmw-usa-announces-compensations-for-customers-affected-by-the-2014-r1200rt-recall-82873.html

www.ingramcontent.com/pod-product-compliance
Lightning Source LLC
Chambersburg PA
CBHW071810090426
42737CB00012B/2026